A Jewish Book of Comfort

Edited by
Rabbi Charles Middleburgh and
Rabbi Andrew Goldstein

Illustrated by Mark Podwal

CANTERBURY
PRESS
Norwich

First published in 2014 by the Canterbury Press Norwich
Editorial office
3rd Floor, Invicta House,
108–114 Golden Lane,
London EC1Y 0TG, UK

Canterbury Press is an imprint of Hymns Ancient & Modern
Ltd (a registered charity)
13A Hellesdon Park Road, Norwich,
Norfolk NR6 5DR, UK

www.canterburypress.co.uk

British Library Cataloguing in Publication data

A catalogue record for this book is available
from the British Library

978 1 84825 721 4

Typeset by Regent Typesetting
Printed and bound by
ScandBook AB Sweden

Contents

iii

The Editors

Andrew Goldstein and Charles Middleburgh have collaborated on writing liturgies for almost thirty years and, in 2003, edited *Machzor Ruach Chadashah*, the High Holy Day prayer book for Liberal Judaism. Andrew is President of Liberal Judaism, Emeritus Rabbi of Northwood and Pinner Liberal Synagogue, and Rabbinic Advisor to the European Union for Progressive Judaism. Charles is the former Executive Director of Liberal Judaism, has served congregations in Britain, Ireland and continental Europe and is the Director of Studies at Leo Baeck College in London.

Acknowledgements

We are most grateful to Mark Podwal who created the artwork for our book.

Although Mark may have been best known initially for his drawings in *The New York Times*, he is the author and illustrator of numerous books. Most of these works – Podwal's own as well as those he has illustrated for others – typically focus on Jewish legend, history and tradition. His art is represented in the collections of the Metropolitan Museum of Art, and the Victoria and Albert Museum, among many others. Though living in New York he is a frequent visitor to Prague and has designed ritual fabrics for the Altneuschul and other synagogues. He recently opened, in Terezin, a major exhibition of his paintings and drawings on the persecution of the Jews. The drawings in this book are inspired by his attachment to Czech Jewry and Israel. The revival of the Jewish community in the Czech Republic should be a source of comfort to us all.

The images by Mark Podwal in our book include a range of Jewish symbols, e.g. the Torah Scroll, Seven-branched candelabrum, Hebrew Zodiac, Lion of Judah and the Ten Commandments; they celebrate the inspiration he gets from regular visits to the city of Prague, with its rich Jewish cultural and spiritual history.

The traditional greeting to mourners is 'May God give you comfort, amongst the mourners of Zion and Jerusalem'.

This is reflected in the cover image, the rose being a symbol of beauty, life, and hope.

We are deeply grateful to our dear friend Beverley Taylor who typed our first draft.

We express our appreciation for the support and help we have received from Christine Smith, Publishing Director, Rebecca Goldsmith, Editorial and Rights Administrator, and Josie Gunn, Sales and Marketing Controller at Canterbury Press.

Above all we must express our gratitude and love to our wives, Sharon and Gilly, who have supported and sustained us on many occasions in our rabbinic and personal lives: they have been a source of wisdom, strength and comfort in the most challenging of times.

The Editors

For the two Elizabeths in my life:
my dear mother
and
Elizabeth Toogood
whose words of wisdom and compassion
have been a true source of comfort to me

CHM

For Sharon
who has dedicated herself to comforting the bereaved
and
Aaron and Ruth
who walk in their parents' footsteps

AG

Introduction

נחמו נחמו עמי אמר אלהיכם

Be comforted, be comforted my people, says your God.

Whether you are a person of faith or not, there are always moments in every human life when we need to find sources of comfort, to sustain us through times of anxiety, disappointment or pain, of loss or bereavement.

Throughout the millennia of Jewish history, from the Hebrew Bible to modern times, Jewish sages have written and spoken words of encouragement, reassurance and hope.

In the pages of this anthology we present a selection of poems, psalms and meditations from all periods of the Jewish past and present that we hope will provide food for thought, and words of comfort at the difficult moments in every human life. We have reproduced these passages in the English of their time as we hope that a variety of styles will give added meaning to readers across the generations.

We know well that some of the passages we have chosen are challenging, indeed on an initial reading they may seem distressing rather than comforting, even harsh: we have included them because our rabbinic experience in congregations has taught us that the value of some texts lies not in the fact that they wrap the reader in a warm embrace but that they stimulate the emotions, and that can be a cathartic, healing process too. Besides, confronting a reality that you might otherwise choose to deny, or the pain of which you might seek to avoid, can be a vital step in finding the comfort and encouragement you seek to begin your life again.

We hope that this collection of readings will provide solace to those in need, encourage a realisation that life is almost always worth living, however hard it seems, most especially when that which is most precious is taken away from us, and we feel that our hold on life has slipped.

It has been our separate privilege, and occasionally struggle, to share with congregants some of the darkest and most challenging moments in human life, and we have drawn strength and hope from the many examples of human fortitude and optimism that have inspired us when our own lives took a turn for the worse.

We have also been fortunate that our collaborative immersion in Jewish liturgy, and the creation of Jewish prayer books, over the last thirty-two years has exposed us to a wider range of Jewish literature and Jewish wisdom than we might otherwise have encountered, which has inspired us to create this book of comfort.

Rabbi Dr Andrew Goldstein
Rabbi Dr Charles H. Middleburgh

Most of the biblical texts used in this anthology are based on the New Revised Standard Version, 1995 (NRSV) or the Jewish Publication Society Tanakh, 1999 (JPS) translations of the Hebrew Bible: some are in gender specific English. In one or two cases, for subjective reasons of aesthetics, we have chosen to use the King James Bible.

The Pain of Life

From Psalm 31

Take pity on me, O God, I am in distress.
Grief wastes away my eyes, my throat, my inmost parts.

For my life is worn out with sorrow, my years with sighs;
my strength yields under misery, my bones are wasting
    away.
I am contemptible, loathsome to my neighbours, to my
    friends a thing of fear.

Those who see me in the street hurry past me;
I am forgotten, as good as dead in their hearts, something
    discarded.

Psalm 31.10–13

The Meaning of Life

Life ultimately means taking the responsibility to find the right answer to its problems and to fulfil the tasks which it constantly sets for each individual.

These tasks, and therefore the meaning of life, differ from man to man, and from moment to moment. Thus it is impossible to define the meaning of life in a general way. Questions about the meaning of life can never be answered by sweeping statements. 'Life' does not mean something vague, but something very real and concrete, just as life's tasks are also very real and concrete. They form man's destiny, which is different and unique for each individual. No man and no destiny can be compared with any other man or any other destiny. No situation repeats itself, and each situation calls for a different response. Sometimes the situation in which a man finds himself may require him to shape his own fate by action. At other times it is more advantageous for him to make use of an opportunity for contemplation and to realize assets in this way. Sometimes man may be required simply to accept fate, to bear his cross. Every situation is distinguished by its uniqueness, and there is always only one right answer to the problem posed by the situation at hand.

When a man finds that it is his destiny to suffer, he will have to accept his suffering as his task; his single and unique task. He will have to acknowledge the fact that even in suffering he is unique and alone in the universe. No one can relieve him of his suffering or suffer in his place. His unique opportunity lies in the way in which he bears his burden.

Viktor E. Frankl

From Psalm 102

A prayer of the destitute who is faint and pours forth his
plea before the Eternal One.

O God, hear my prayer; let my cry come before You.
Do not hide Your face from me in my time of trouble; turn
Your ear to me; when I cry, answer me speedily.

For my days are vanished like smoke and my bones are
charred like a hearth.
My body is stricken and withered like grass; too wasted to
eat my food; on account of my despair my bones show
through my skin.
I am like a pelican in the wilderness, a tawny owl among
the ruins.
I lie awake; I am like a lone bird upon a roof.
For I have eaten ashes like bread and mixed my drink with
tears.
My days are like a lengthening shadow; I wither like grass.
But You, Eternal One, are enthroned forever; Your fame
endures throughout the ages.

Psalm 102.1–10, 12–13

Dark is the Night

The night is dark
And I am blind.
The wind tears the stick
from my hand.

Bare is my sack,
empty my heart.
And both are useless,
Too heavy a weight.

3

I hear the touch
of someone's hand:
Allow me to carry
your heavy load.

Together we go.
The world is dark.
I carry the sack,
and he ... my heart.

M. Leivik Halpin

The Pain of Job

Afterward, Job began to speak and cursed the day of his birth. Job spoke up and said:

Perish the day on which I was born
And the night it was announced,
'A male has been conceived!'
May that day be darkness;
May God above have no concern for it;
May light not shine on it;
May darkness and deep gloom reclaim it;
May a pall lie over it;
May what blackens the day terrify it.
May obscurity carry off that night;
May it not be counted among the days of the year;
May it not appear in any of its months;
May that night be desolate;
May no sound of joy be heard in it;
May its twilight stars remain dark;
May it hope for light and have none;
May it not see the glimmerings of the dawn –
Because it did not block my mother's womb,
And hide trouble from my eyes.

Why did I not die at birth,
Expire as I came forth from the womb?
Why were there knees to receive me,
Or breasts for me to suck?
For now would I be lying in repose, asleep and at rest,
With the world's kings and counsellors who rebuild ruins
    for themselves,
Or with nobles who possess gold and who fill their houses
    with silver.
Or why was I not like a buried stillbirth,
Like babies who never saw the light?
There the wicked cease from troubling;
There rest those whose strength is spent.
Prisoners are wholly at ease;
They do not hear the taskmaster's voice.
Small and great alike are there,
And the slave is free of his master.

Why does He give light to the sufferer
And life to the bitter in spirit;
To those who wait for death but it does not come,
Who search for it more than treasure,
Who rejoice to exultation,
And are glad to reach the grave;
To the man who has lost his way;
Whom God has hedged about?
My groaning serves as my bread;
My roaring pours forth as water.
For what I feared has overtaken me;
What I dreaded has come upon me.
I had no repose, no quiet, no rest,
And trouble came.

Job 3.1–7, 9–26

No Easy Answer

The Book of Job, which describes its protagonist who is afflicted with the most terrible suffering as the most righteous of men, raises to an intense and painful level the problem of why a just God allows human suffering. Throughout the book, the question that Job repeatedly asks, and which God never answers, is: Why has such evil befallen me? When the Lord does finally respond to Job 'out of the whirlwind', it is with His own rhetorical questions:

> Where were you when I established the world?
> Tell me, if you know so much,
> Who drafted its dimension? Do you know? ...
> Did you ever command forth a morning? ...

> *Job 38.4–5, 12*

How can one explain God's response? God never tells Job why he, or any human being suffers. God is God is basically what He says, and who are we to assume that we can understand everything? Who 'established the world', human beings or God? As a medieval Hebrew proverb teaches, 'If I knew God, I'd be God.' Admittedly, that may not be a response we, or Job, hope for, but *what* answer would we desire? If God is God and humans are humans, is there any other possible answer than the one Job receives?

God concludes with the challenge: 'Will the contender with God yield?' (40.2). And Job, who throughout the book has sought a divine response, no longer has questions and challenges for God: 'I am small, how can I answer You? My hand I lay on my mouth' (40.4).

Perhaps the Book of Job's most important teaching is that the 'why' of human suffering is, and always will be, beyond human knowledge or understanding.

Joseph Telushkin

Spare Those I Love

My God, do not take my loved ones from me
Do not let me be left alone!
Lonely people, their heart is hard
Like the bush in the wilderness.
They eat their bread in toil
With the bitter salt,
Until their tooth is set on edge
Until their voice goes hoarse
And is made dumb and unable to say: my God,
Do not take my loved ones from me,
Do not let me be left alone!

Tuviah Ruebner

The Great Sad One

The Almighty has dealt bitterly with me

That I did not believe in Him until my punishment,

Till He welled up in my tears, from the midst of my
 wounds.

And behold – He also is very lonely,

And he also lacks someone to confess to,

In whose arms He might sob His unbearable misery.

And this God walks about, without a body, without blood,

And His grief is double the grief of flesh,

Flesh that can warm another body or a third,

That can sit and smoke a cigarette,

And drink coffee and wine,

And sleep and dream until the sun –

For Him, it is impossible, for He is God.

Robert Mezey

Gray Good-Bye

You've become inaccessible to me.
Love is luck, anyway, and we had our good days.
Too much bitterness is for people
in their twenties, for sure,
so we'll save that bit of anguish.
We're too bright to speak of breaking hearts;
we knew all that from our rock and roll years,
and we'd be embarrassed to weep.
So let's leave it as it is:
a sophisticated parting of the ways,
two adults, muted by the psychology of differences,
going our own roads later in life,
not without sadness or fatigue,
dulled a shade by another brush with mystery.

Don't go just yet.

Yes – go.
I sense tears,
and I would be ashamed.

Danny Siegel

8

The Storms of Life

In my great need for light I look to You. Eternal God, help me to feel Your presence even when dark shadows fall upon me. When my own weakness and the storms of life hide You from my sight, help me to know that You have not deserted me. Uphold me with the comfort of Your love! Give me trust, O God, give me peace, and give me light. May my heart find its rest in You.

Israel I. Mattuck

Swim or Drown

It is written, '*and Noah walked with God*'. This signifies that he secluded himself with his Creator and avoided human company. Or else it may signify that he was so advanced in the practice of solitude that even when he was among men these did not distract him, for they were as non-existent in his eyes ... A man in the company of others is like unto one who has fallen into the sea – unless he swims well he will be drowned; but if he flees society and secludes himself with his Creator, then he is like one in a boat, saved and in communion with God.

Elazar Azikri

Fear and Loneliness

There are times when each of us feels lost or alone, when we seem to be adrift and forsaken, unable to reach our fellow-men, or to be reached by them. And there are days and nights when all existence seems to lack purpose; our lives mere sparks in an indifferent cosmos, that flicker for a brief moment and are extinguished. Fear and loneliness enter into the soul. None of us is immune from doubt and fear; no one escapes times when all seems dark and senseless. Then, at the ebb-tide of the spirit, the soul cries out and reaches for companionship.

Eternal God, we humbly ask Your help, for our need is great. Our days fly past in quick succession, and we cannot look back without regret or ahead without misgiving. We seek to understand the mysteries of sin and evil, but in vain. When suffering and death strike those we love, our pain and anger embitter us, and we question Your justice. Our faith fails us, and we forget that we are Your children. O God, make Your presence felt among us.

Siddur Lev Chadash

Faith ...

'Faith is not an insurance but a constant effort, a constant listening to the eternal voice.' Abraham Joshua Heschel believed that faith was not something that was intrinsically present for human beings, but that it came from an active search for God, and a conscious decision to lead a useful and ethical life, guided by the teachings of Judaism and motivated by doing God's will.

Editors, inspired by A. J. Heschel

Adon Olam

Lord of the world, He reigned alone
    While yet the universe was naught.
    When by His will all things were wrought,
Then first His sov'reign name was known.

And when the All shall cease to be,
   In dread lone splendour He shall reign.
   He was, He is, He shall remain
In glorious eternity.

For He is one, no second shares
   His nature or His loneliness;
   Unending and beginningless,
All strength is His, all sway He bears.

He is the living God to save,
   My rock while sorrow's toils endure,
   My banner and my stronghold sure,
The cup of life where'er I crave.

I place my soul within His palm
   Before I sleep as when I wake,
   And though my body I forsake,
Rest in the Lord in fearless calm.

Israel Zangwill

From Psalm 4

Answer me when I call, God of my vindication,
You gave me space when I was in distress.
Be gracious to me, and hear my prayer.

Safe and sound I will then lie down and sleep in peace;
for you alone, Eternal, make me lie down in safety.

Psalm 4.2, 9

2

Patience and Fortitude

Why?

I do not know how to ask You, Ruler of the world, and
even if I did know, I could not bear to do it. How could I
venture to ask You why everything happens as it does, why
are we driven from one exile into another, why our foes are
allowed to torment us so. But in the Haggadah, the parent
of the child 'who does not yet know how to ask' is told, 'It is
incumbent upon you to disclose it to the child.' Adonai, am I
not your child? I do not ask You to reveal the secret of Your
ways – I could not stand it! But show me one thing. Show
me what this very moment means to me, what it demands
of me, what You, God, are telling me through my life at this
moment. I do not ask You to tell me why I suffer, but only
whether I suffer for Your sake.

Levi Yitzchak of Berditchev

Give Me Courage

O Lord, let me feel Your presence. Give me courage to live in accordance with Your will, even when shadows fall upon me. When my own weaknesses, and the storms of life, hide You from my sight, take me by the hand and teach me that You are near to me at all times, and especially when I strive to live a truer, gentler and nobler life. Give me trust, O Lord; give me peace, and give me light. May my heart find its rest in You.

Liberal Jewish Prayer Book

I Shall Live

The morning after I received the news that I had cancer and that I was going to have surgery, I went to shul [synagogue]. It was Shemini Atzeret [a festival], and I did what I always do on Shemini Atzeret, which is go to shul. Concentration was hard because there were so many thoughts and feelings – everything coming at once, hard to organize or make any coherence out of the whole mishmash.

But I got to Hallel, the special Psalms of praise we add on holidays ... I reached the verse that says ... 'I shall not die but live, and I will tell of the works of the Lord' – or loosely translated, 'I will tell stories about God'. As I read that verse, I knew at that moment that it expressed the content of my heart. I wasn't going to die, I was going to live and I was going to live to tell about God. Walking to the synagogue that morning, I wasn't thinking of that verse. But when I read it that morning in shul, it helped me to express what I was feeling, the determination that I was going to live and not die.

Elana Kanter

A Prayer

Teach me, teach me how
To deal with the world, O Lord!
And how I may transform
Evil into good.

If a wild beast lurks
In our humanity,
Let me turn it toward
A mild humility.

I've seen a trainer in
The circus tame a tiger;
Seen him de-fang a snake.
Lord, let me be wiser.

Bless me with patience, too,
And make me iron hard
That I may show mankind
At least such wonders, Lord.

Abraham Reisen

In Times of Darkness

In times of darkness when my heart is grieved,
When despair besieges my mind
And my days are a weariness of living –
Then is my life like the flower that struggles to grow
Where no ray of sun ever penetrates;
Then is my spirit pent up within me
And my soul is shut in like a night of darkness.

When such darkness overtakes me, O God,
Fortify my mind with trust in life.
Let not the blight of futility engulf my existence.
Knit up the sinews of my strength still to struggle.
Drive on the will within me to ceaseless exertion
Until my powers break through my mortal toils
And blaze forth with the strength of Thy Spirit.

Jacob L. Halevi

From Psalm 16

I have set You, Eternal God, always before me;
You are ever near me; I shall not be moved.

Therefore my heart is glad and my soul can rejoice,
for I am safe in your presence.

You will not abandon me to death nor send Your servant
to destruction.

You show me the path of life.
In Your presence is fullness of joy;
And in Your shelter, happiness for ever more.

Psalm 16.8–11

When Bad Things Happen

God does not cause our misfortunes. Some are caused by
bad luck, some are caused by bad people, and some are
simply an inevitable consequence of our being human and
being mortal, living in a world of inflexible natural laws.
The painful things that happen to us are not punishments
for our misbehaviour, nor are they in any way part of some

grand design on God's part. Because the tragedy is not God's will, we need not feel hurt or betrayed by God when tragedy strikes. We can turn to Him for help in overcoming it, precisely because we can tell ourselves that God is as outraged as we are ...

Bad things that happen to us in our lives do not have a meaning when they happen to us. They do not happen for any good reason which would cause us to accept them willingly. But we can give them a meaning. We can redeem these tragedies from senselessness by imposing meaning on them. The question we should be asking is not, 'Why did this happen to me? What did I do to deserve this?' That is really an unanswerable, pointless question. A better question would be 'Now that this has happened to me what am I going to do about it ...?'

Harold S. Kushner

When All is Dark

When all within is dark,
    And former friends misprize;
From them I turn to Thee,
    And find Love in Thine eyes.
When all within is dark,
    And I my soul despise;
From me I turn to Thee,
    And find love in Thine eyes.

When all Thy face is dark,
    And Thy just angers rise;
From Thee I turn to Thee,
    And find love in Thine eyes.

Israel Abrahams, based on Solomon ibn Gabirol

Psalm 13

How long, O God? Will you forget me for ever?
How long will you hide your face from me?

How long must I bear pain in my soul,
and have sorrow in my heart all day long?
How long shall my enemy be exalted over me?

Consider and answer me, Eternal my God!
God give light to my eyes, or I will sleep the sleep of death,

and my enemy will say, 'I have prevailed';
my foes will rejoice because I am shaken.

But I trusted in your steadfast love, my heart shall rejoice
in your salvation.

I will sing to the Eternal who has dealt bountifully with me.

Editors

3

Illness

Loss of Health

Perhaps more than any other event
the loss of health
raises the most urgent issues
about
good and evil,
reward and punishment,
of why terrible things happen to a loved one.

Your religion may provide you
with a spiritual philosophy
that helps you make some sense of
sickness and health.

Beware.

Religion can be hazardous to your health,
when you believe you haven't prayed hard
enough,
and punishment is linked with illness.

Religion then becomes a tool
for denial of real emotions and
keeps you from releasing feelings of
helplessness, guilt, anger.
A mature, forgiving, open faith
encourages expression
allows your angry cry to heaven –
  'How could you, God!'

Religion offers no absolute answers,
no guarantee of special treatment,
no extended length of time for your beloved.

For many,
faith *does*
help its believers
to accept the unacceptable,
and to ennoble
ignoble misfortune.

Earl A. Grollman

What Not to Say

A visitor came to see a sick man and asked him what ailed him. After the sick man told him, the visitor said: 'Oh, my father died of the same disease.'

The sick man became extremely distressed, but the visitor said, 'Don't worry, I'll pray to God to heal you.'

To which the sick man answered: 'And when you pray, add that I may be spared visits from any more stupid people.'

Zevi Hirsch Edelman

My Last Cancer Treatment

In 2003 I suffered a grand mal seizure followed by the diagnosis of a brain tumour.

I had the strange, surreal experience of hearing my congregants' shock that this could happen to the family of the Rabbi – as though professional piety was a shield against disease. As though God played favourites.

Right before my brain surgery I appeared in front of the congregation and asked them for their patience and their prayers. Three years later I was standing before them, bald. I witnessed the realisation in their eyes that there are no guarantees, no protected people. No one was safe.

David Wolpe

Prayer for Healing

In sickness I turn to You, O God, and seek Your help. You create the healing powers that flow in the bloodstream of every living creature. You are the Source of the knowledge and skill of doctors and nurses, and of the dedication that prompts them to give of their best. From You comes the comforting care of my loved ones, and the tranquillity of spirit which I and they need at this time of distress.

And so I pray: May all these forces combine to speed my recovery. Let not my sickness weaken my faith in You, nor diminish my concern for the well-being of others, but let me gain from it a deeper appreciation of life and its blessings, and a fuller sympathy for all who suffer.

May it be Your will, Eternal One, our God and God of our ancestors, speedily to grant a perfect healing, of body and mind, to me and all who are sick. I praise you, O God, the Source of healing.

Siddur Lev Chadash

As One Approaches Surgery (or Crisis)

God, you are with me in my moments of strength and of weakness. You know the trembling of my heart as the turning point draws near.

Grant wisdom and skill to the mind and hands of those who will operate on me, and those who assist them. Grant that I may return to fullness of life and wholeness of strength, not for my sake alone but for those about me. Enable me to complete my days on earth with dignity and purpose. May I awaken to know the breadth of Your healing power now and evermore.

My spirit I commit to You, my body, too, and all I prize;
Both when I sleep and when I wake, You are with me;
I shall not fear.

Chaim Stern

Keeping Perspective

O God, how helpless I feel! I am so dependent on my phys-
ician, my nurses, and all those who work in the hospital. I
need medication to alleviate my discomfort and pain, and to
help me rest. I am not as strong as I was, I'm not as free as I
was, I don't feel as well as I did.

But help me, O God, not to lose perspective. Keep me aware
of the strength I do possess, what I am able to do, and the
blessings that still are mine. Amen.

Chaim Stern

The Long Days

My God and God of all generations, in my great need I pour
out my heart to You. The days and weeks of suffering are
hard to endure. In my struggle, I reach out for the help that
You alone can give. Let me feel that You are near, and that
Your care enfolds me. Rouse in me the strength to overcome
fear and anxiety, and brighten my spirit with the assurance
of Your love. May I show appreciation of the care I am
receiving, and help me to help my loved ones in their striving
to encourage me. Let the healing power within me, which
comes from You, give me strength to recover, that I and all
who love me may rejoice.

Gates of Healing

Out of the Depths

A Song of Ascents

Out of the depths I cry to you, Eternal One.

O God, hear my voice!
Let Your ears be attentive to the voice of my supplications!

If You, Eternal One, should count iniquities,
O God, who could stand?
But there is forgiveness with You, so that You may be
    revered.
I wait for the Eternal One, my soul waits, and in God's
    word I have hope;
I wait more eagerly for the Eternal One,
more than those who watch for the morning,
more than those who watch for the morning.
O Israel, hope in the Eternal One!
For with God there is steadfast love,
and great power to redeem.

Psalm 130

For Those Living with a Chronic Illness

May the one who blessed our ancestors, Sarah, Rebecca, Leah
and Rachel, Abraham, Isaac, and Jacob, bless all those with
chronic illness and help them to endure. Lift up their spirits
and give them strength to embrace both joy and sorrow.
Help their friends and caregivers know their own strengths
and weaknesses, and the common humanity shared with
those to whom they offer comfort. We remember Jacob's
limp, Moses' speech impediment, Leah's weak eyes, and all

that each contributed. Grant courage, faith, and joy to all
who bear chronic illness and to all who love them. Amen.

Jeffrey Lilly

To Wake Up in the Hospital Early in the Morning

To wake up in hospital early in the morning
To the prospect of a pointless day, and feel
Set in the flesh of your heart
The teeth of despair gnaw and pierce,
Through the eye of the minutes with weary hand
To feed the rotten thread of life
Over and over again,
What do the healthy know of such an hour?

In the hospital now the day grows dark,
Already night rules;
Softly in its wake descend
Reconcilement and peace.
The doctor's footsteps are heard in the hall,
Gently the comforting hand
touches yours,
What do the healthy know of such an hour?

Rachel

Send out Your Light

As a hind longs for flowing streams,
so does my soul long for You, O God.

My soul thirsts for God, for the living God.
When shall I come to behold the face of God?

Letting Go

Give me strength
That I may continue my efforts
On behalf of others who are under my care.
And help me grow in wisdom and judgment.
As I dedicate myself to enhancing life,
Let me humbly accept
That there is a time
We must each let go of living.

Adonai natan v'Adonai lakakh,
Yehi Shem Adonai mevorach.
The Eternal has given, the Eternal has taken back;
Blessed be the Eternal.
Shema Yisrael
Adonai eloheinu
Adonai echad

Nancy Flam

Psalm 91

You who live in the shelter of the Most High,
    who abide in the shadow of the Almighty,
will say to the Lord, 'My refuge and my fortress;
    my God, in whom I trust.'
For He will deliver you from the snare of the fowler
    and from the deadly pestilence;
He will cover you with His pinions, and under His wings
    you will find refuge;
    His faithfulness is a shield and buckler.
You will not fear the terror of the night,
    or the arrow that flies by day,
or the pestilence that stalks in darkness,
    or the destruction that wastes at noonday.

73

Because you have made the Lord your refuge,
   the Most High your dwelling-place,
no evil shall befall you,
   no scourge come near your tent.

For He will command His angels concerning you
   to guard you in all your ways.
On their hands they will bear you up,
   so that you will not dash your foot against a stone.
You will tread on the lion and the adder,
   the young lion and the serpent you will trample under foot.

Those who love me, I will deliver;
   I will protect those who know my name.
When they call to me, I will answer them;
   I will be with them in trouble, I will rescue them and
      honour them.
With long life I will satisfy them,
   and show them my salvation.

(NRSV)

Life and Death

To the living –
Death is a wound. Its name is grief.
Its companion is loneliness.
Whenever it comes – whatever its guise,
Even when there are no tears –
Death is a wound.

But death belongs to life –
As night belongs to day
As darkness belongs to light
As shadows belong to substance –
As the fallen leaf to the tree,
Death belongs to life.

It is not our purpose to live forever.
It is only our purpose to live.
It is no added merit that a man lives long.
It is of merit only that his life is good.

Alvin I. Fine

On his deathbed, Rabbi Simha Bunam of Przysucha said to
his wife, 'Why are you crying? My whole life was only that
I might learn how to die.'

Chassidic

My Grandmother

When my grandmother died
The birds sang.
The whole world with her kind deeds
And her good heart rang.

When they lifted my grandmother from the bed,
And laid her on the floor,
Everybody wept, because
The kind old lady was no more.

My grandfather walked up and down the room,
With anger in his eye,
Because he had promised grandmother,
He would be first to die.

When they bore her into the town,
All the Christian folk cried,
And the Greek Catholic Priest lamented,
That such a good woman had died.

Only when the Shamash took his knife,
To cut in their clothes the mourning slash,
My uncles and my father cried aloud,
Like prisoners under the lash.

Moyshe Kulbak

How We Bury

Burial is the final act of love, the ultimate gesture of *kavod ha-met*, honouring the dead. The rabbi explains that it is not for strangers to bury our dead, but for each and every one of us to provide the blanket of earth for the final rest. You are taken to the grave and handed a shovel. As difficult as it is, you fill the shovel with earth and empty it into the grave.

The dirt hits the top of the coffin with a thud, and that thud sends a shudder through your whole body, which you will long remember. You stand aside as your family and close friends take turns carrying out this last *mitzvah* – this *mitzvah* for which there will be no repayment, no reward except the knowledge that you have done a good deed, that you have brought the deceased to a final resting place. Friends approach you with hugs and words of condolence. They form two lines with an aisle between them. And as you walk by, they offer you the ancient words of hope and consolation: 'May God comfort you, together with all those who mourn for Zion and Jerusalem.' You reach the car and collapse in tears in the back seat, numbed and exhausted. As you leave the cemetery you take one last, long look back, knowing that with this ending comes a beginning. The funeral is over, the mourning can now begin.

Ron Wolfson

From a Mother to Her Girls

The morning you wake to bury me
you'll wonder what to wear.
The sun may be shining, or maybe it will rain;
it may be winter. Or not.
You'll say to your self, black, aren't you
    supposed to
wear black? Then you will remember all the
    times we went
together to buy clothes: the prom,
    homecoming,
just another pair of jeans,
another sweater, another pair of shoes.
    I called you my Barbie dolls.
You will remember how I loved to dress you.
How beautiful you were in my eyes.

The morning you wake to bury me
you will look in the mirror in disbelief.
You'll reach for some makeup. Or not.
    And you won't believe that
this is the morning you will bury your mother.
But it is. And as you gaze into that mirror
    You will
shed a tear. Or not. But look. Look carefully,
for hiding in your expression, you will find mine.
You will see me in your eyes, in the way you
    laugh.
You will feel me when you think of God,
and of love and struggle.

Look into the mirror and you will see me in
    a look, or in

the way you hold your mouth or stand, a little
bent, or maybe straight.
But you will see me.

So let me tell you one last time, before you
    dress,
what to wear. Put on any old thing. Black or
    red, skirt or pants.
Despite what I told you all these years, it doesn't
    really matter.
Because as I told you all these years, you are
    beautiful the way you are.
Dress yourself in honour and dignity.
Dress yourself in confidence and self-love.
Wear a sense of obligation to do for this world,
for you are one of the lucky ones and there is
    so much to do, to fix.
Take care of each other,
take care of your heart, of your soul.
Talk to God.
Wear humility and compassion.

When you wake up to bury me,
put on a strong sense of self, courage, and
    understanding.
I am sorry. Forgive me. I am sorry.
Stand at my grave clothed in a gown of
    forgiveness,
dressed like an angel would be, showing
    compassion
and unconditional love.
For at that very moment, all that will be left
    of me to give is love.
Love.

Karyn Kedar

8

A Coda: Death Before Their Time

On the Death of the Young

David prayed to God for his child; he fasted, and lay all night upon the ground. The elders of his house tried to raise him from the ground, but he would not rise, nor would he eat food with them. On the seventh day the child died. The servants of King David feared to tell him that the child was dead, for they reasoned: 'While his child was still alive, he did not listen to us when we spoke to him. How, then, can we tell him that the child is dead? He may do himself some harm.'

When David noticed that his servants were whispering to each other, he realized that the child was dead. Then David asked his servants, 'Is the child dead?' They answered, 'He is dead.' So David arose from the ground and washed and changed his clothes, and he went to the house of the Lord, and he worshipped. Then he went to his own house and, when asked, they set food before him, and he ate. His servants then asked him, 'What is this thing that you have done?' And David replied, 'While the child was still alive, I fasted and I wept, for I said, "Who knows whether the Lord will be gracious to me, that the child will live?" But now he is dead. Why should I fast? Can I bring him back? I shall go to him, but he will not return to me.'

2 Samuel 12.16–23

A Wife's Wisdom

It happened that while Rabbi Meir was teaching in the house of study on a Sabbath afternoon, his two sons died. What did their mother do? She put them both on a couch and spread a sheet over them.

At the end of the Sabbath, Rabbi Meir returned home and asked, 'Where are my sons?' She replied, 'They went to the house of study.' Rabbi Meir said, 'Really? I looked for them there and did not see them.'

Then she gave him the cup for *Havdalah,* and he pronounced the blessings. Again he asked, 'Where are my sons?' She replied, 'They went to such-and-such place and will be back soon.' Then she brought him food. After he had eaten, she said, 'My teacher, I have a question.' Rabbi Meir said, 'What is it?' She said, 'My teacher, a while ago someone came and deposited something with me for safekeeping. Now that person has come back to claim what he left. Should I return it to him or not?' Rabbi Meir said, 'My daughter, is not one who holds a deposit required to return it to its owner?' She said, 'Still, without your opinion, I would not have returned it.'

Then what did she do? She took Rabbi Meir by the hand and led him upstairs to the chamber and brought him to the couch. Then she pulled off the sheet, and he saw his two children lying there dead.

He began to weep and say, 'My sons, my sons, my teachers, my teachers! My sons in the ways of the world but my teachers because you illumined my eyes with your understanding of the Torah.'

Then she said to him: 'My teacher, did you not say to me that we are required to restore to the owner what he gives to us in trust? "The Lord gave, and the Lord has taken back. Blessed be the name of the Lord" (Job 1.21).'

Midrash Proverbs 31.10

Something Precious

Something precious is taken from us, and we think of it as something we have lost, instead of something we have had. We remember only how empty our lives are now, we forget how full and rich they were before; we forget all the many days and years of happiness we lived while the beloved object was still with us. We praise God for our treasures while we have them; we cease to praise Him for them when they are fled. But God never gives; He only lends. What is life itself but a loan?

When God claims His own shall we rebel? Instead of murmuring because He takes our precious things from us, let us be grateful to Him for having spared them to us so long. Let us count the past happy days not as loss, but as gain. We have had them; and, now that they are ended, let us turn the loss to glorious gain – the gain that comes with

new courage, with nobler tasks, with a wider outlook on life
and duty.

Morris Joseph

After a Stillbirth

O Lord our God,
For a time You gave us the hope of a new life,
Placed in us the expectation of a new awakening.
Now, in Your wisdom,
You have taken that hope from us,
Have delayed for reasons known only to You,
The arrival of that new soul into our world.

Lord, we thank You still
For the hope you gave us,
And pray that You may renew in us that hope in time to
    come;
Though the pain of our disappointment is real and deep,
We acknowledge still that You are our God;
You renew Life beyond Death,
You give, and take away,
You hold all our souls in the palm of Your hand.

May it be Your will to give us, once more,
the chance to share with You
in the bringing of new life to this our world;
May it be Your will that we shall be strengthened both by
our hopes and by our disappointments
and learn to love, the more deeply, that which we have.
Blessed are You, Lord, Who shares the sorrow of Your
    creation.

Walter Rothschild

On the Death of His Son Isaac

Father of the child, draw near to mourn,
For God has taken away from you
Your son, your only son,
The son whom you love, Isaac.

I am the man who has seen
Destruction, whose joy has fled.
Alas, I have lost the fruit of my loins,
And it never came into my mind;
For I thought that in my old age
He would be well and strong.
But I have laboured in vain,
I have begotten a son, to dismay me.
For how can my heart be glad
At the death and departure of Isaac?

I shall lament and weep each minute,
And raise a plaintive cry,
When I remember how three years ago
He died in a foreign land;
How he journeyed from place to place,
My soul yearning after him,
Until I brought him back to my home,
While I wept night and day.
How many sorrows befell me!
These are the generations of Isaac!

My friend, take your leave of me.
If you console me, you grieve me.

Do not recall my soul's beloved
Do not compel me to hear his name.
The small fire that was left to me

Fate has quenched. Can it harm me more?
It has overwhelmed me with eternal disaster.
It has taken the delight of my eyes.
My flesh and my heart have reached their end,
Together with the ending of Isaac.

God, in whose hand is all,
Who do your will with all your creatures,
Speak to the distressed heart of a father,
Who has feared your name from the day of his youth.
Rouse your spirit of consolation for him,
And enter into his divided soul.
He taught his beloved to fear you,
To walk in the way of his forbears.
You dictated, while he was still young,
The way for your servant, Isaac.

Abraham ibn Ezra

Bittersweet: In Memory of a Child

Bittersweet
   The struggle to be born,
    To free the infant body from the womb,
    Sever the umbilical cord.

Bittersweet
   The first gasping for air,
    Listening to the heart beat,
    A life lived outside the body of another.

Bittersweet
   Hope revived out of ambiguous prognosis,
    Love clung to in the deepening anxiety.

Bittersweet
> The stilled body.
> Love never forgotten.
> Can the promise be resurrected?

Bittersweet
> May the memory of a life nearly lived,
> Help us look beyond the eclipse,
> Come to new light, new song, new hope.

Harold M. Schulweis

Cold Comfort

When Rabban Yochanan ben Zakkai's son died, his disciples came in to comfort him.

Rabbi Eliezer said, 'Adam had a son who died, yet he was comforted for the loss of him. How do we know? Because it is said, "And Adam knew his wife again, and Adam said, God has provided me with another offspring in place of Abel" (Genesis 4.25). You, too, must be comforted.' Rabban Yochanan said to him: 'Is it not enough that I grieve over my own? Do you have to remind me of Adam's grief?'

Rabbi Joshua came to comfort Rabbi Yochanan and reminded him that 'Job had sons and daughters, all of whom died on one day, and he was comforted for the loss of them'. Rabban Yochanan said to him: 'Is it not enough that I grieve over my own? Do you have to remind me of Job's grief?'

In like manner Rabbi Yose reminded him that Aaron's two sons died on the same day. Rabbi Shimon that King David had a son who died, yet he allowed himself to be comforted. To them all Rabbi Yochanan replied as before.

Then Rabbi Eleazar sat down before him and said, 'May I tell you a parable: To whom may you be likened? To a man with whom the king deposited a precious object. Each and every day the man would weep and cry out, saying, "Woe is me! When will I be safely relieved of this trust?" You too, Master, had a son: he studied the Torah, the Prophets, the Writings; he studied *Mishnah*, *Halachah* and *Aggadah*, and departed from this world without sin. You should be comforted because you have returned unimpaired what was given you in trust.'

Rabban Yochanan said to him, 'Eleazar, my son, you have comforted me the way men should give comfort!'

Avot deRabbi Natan 14.6

For Parents Who Mourn a Child

'Out of the depths I call to You, Eternal One.
O God hearken to my voice.' (Psalm 130.1–2)

We looked for joy,
and now suddenly,
birds sing,
but not our child.

We looked for life
and now, suddenly,
trees bloom,
but not our child.

How our laughter has turned into grief, our mirth to tears!
Hope was full within us; now it is turned to sorrow and
    lamentation.

O God, from You we come, to You we go, You have been
    our refuge in all generations.
Take our grief, and make us whole again, as it is written:
'You shall forget your misery, and remember it only as
    waters that pass away.' (Job 11.16)

Chaim Stern

Suicide

I cannot see you, feel you, touch you ...
... you have ripped yourself away from me
torn a rent in my life that seems beyond repair.

I need to understand, I need to find a way
of changing my rage at your selfishness
to grief at your loss.

I need to be able to reach beyond the pain,
beyond the shame at my own failure to give you
what you needed. But I confess I do not know
how to start, how to overcome the raw sense of
amputation, of catastrophic loss
that marks your absence from my life.

How can I praise or magnify or extol
the God who let you exercise your
freewill to your own destruction?

How can the Maker of Peace give peace to
my devastated soul?

I have no answers, no meaningful responses
to your death, only questions. I do not know how I will
    survive
this terrible blow.

I ache for the love I shall never feel again,
I yearn for the voice I shall never hear again;
so I shall reach for the love I have still,
the understanding I have still,
the shared memory that others have of you,
the shared disbelief that your vibrant presence
is stilled.

O God, full of a compassion I cannot yet feel,
help me to find an understanding that
I can accept, and strengthen me to
touch the memories that are now
beyond me – and having touched them
to live again,
your absence now a presence, your
memory once again, a blessing.

Charles Middleburgh

9

Grieving

Psalm 121

A Song of Ascents

I will lift up mine eyes unto the hills, from whence cometh
    my help.
My help *cometh* from the Lord, which made heaven and
    earth.
He will not suffer thy foot to be moved: he that keepeth
    thee will not slumber.
Behold, he that keepeth Israel shall neither slumber nor
    sleep.
The Lord *is* thy keeper: the Lord is thy shade upon thy
    right hand.
The sun shall not smite thee by day, nor the moon by night.
The Lord shall preserve thee from all evil: he shall preserve
    thy soul.
The Lord shall preserve thy going out and thy coming in
    from this time forth, and even for evermore.

                               (King James Version)

All go to the house of mourning and each weeps over his own sorrow.

Joshua ibn Shuaib, Olat Shabbat 53

Peace of Mind: Grief's Slow Wisdom

We must face grief without any expectation of miraculous healing, but with the knowledge that if we are courageous and resolute we can live as our loved ones would wish us to live, not empty, morose, self-centred, and self-pitying, but as brave and undismayed servants of the greater life. Rabbinic wisdom teaches this approach to grief in the following passage: 'When the second Temple in Jerusalem was destroyed many Jews began to withdraw from life and sank into a state of depressed mourning for the sons and daughters of Israel that had perished and also for the Temple that had gone up in smoke. They refused to eat and to drink.' Rabbi Joshua said to them: 'My sons, I know that it is impossible not to mourn, but to mourn excessively is forbidden.' Why? Because that great Jewish sage felt that we human beings must think not only of the past but of the future. We are commanded by our religion to be the servants of life as long as we live.

Joshua Loth Liebman

The Law Sets the Limits

One must not grieve excessively for the dead. Whoever weeps more than the law requires must be weeping for something else. Rather, let one accept the schedule set down by the sages: three days for weeping, seven for lamenting, thirty for mourning.

Shulchan Arukh Yoreh Deah 394

Three Laws for Governing Grief

One of the greatest illusions about human nature is that the expression of grief will lead to a breakdown. *Quite the reverse*. No one has ever broken down nervously through the legitimate expression of an emotional reaction. The distortion, the concealment, the denial of our normal human feelings may well prove the breeding ground of delayed breakdowns. The truth is that we human beings are tough organisms and can withstand much rough handling. How absurd is that notion current in modern society that men and women must be safeguarded, coddled, and shielded against emotional outbursts. It is not those outbursts which harm the human organism, but the complete avoidance of them, which scars and tears the fabric of the inner soul.

A second new truth about the grief situation is this: *we must learn how to extricate ourselves from the bondage of the physical existence and coexistence of the loved one*. A husband and wife who have lived and worked together harmoniously, sharing with each other the successes and failures of the common struggle, inevitably build their hopes upon the assumption of the continuity of the marital pattern. The death of one of the partners leaves an aching void and a gaping hole in the fabric of life. Death comes quickly, but it cannot quickly erase the expectancies of a lifetime from the slate of memory and the surviving partner yearns in vain for the presence of the comrade. The achievement of mental balance will be expedited if the pain of loneliness and loss be courageously accepted and lived through rather than evaded and avoided. Words have their own magic potency, and human speech has the most blessed ability to compound balm and medicine for the overburdened heart. It is only by speaking to others of the loss and of the magnitude of that bereavement that gradually the pain itself proves bearable.

Joshua Loth Liebman

For My Mother

Deep is the spring in wood and field
The grass is rich and thick and deep
The grain proclaims its promised yield,
In waves of green the green fires creep,
The fires of spring that spread and glow
And cover all the earth, and grow.
Mindless, the waxy leaves uncurl
Heartless, your garden comes to bloom
Tulips, scarlet and white, unfurl
Without recall or thought or gloom,
But you have gone from life and spring
You cannot see nor work nor sing.

Now grief enlarges like a tree
And branches into every hour,
Heavy and green, grief grows in me
Deepens its roots, bursts into flower,
Spreads like the green fires of spring,
And I am soil for this burning thing.

I stand to recite the proper prayer
'Extolled and magnified is the Lord',
But you mock me on the empty air,
Though you cannot hear nor speak a word
You cannot knit, your hands are still,

Yet I know your strength, your mind, your will.
Why did you go when warmth was in the air
Before you saw your trillium once again?
The grief for my father is old and rare
But now for you I grieve as I began,
Torn from you, weeping, with sobbing breath,
In the bitter green season of your death.

Ruth F. Brin

The Five Stages of Grief

The night I lost you
someone pointed me towards
the Five Stages of Grief.
Go that way, they said,
it's easy, like learning to climb
stairs after amputation.
And so I climbed.
Denial was first.
I sat down at breakfast
carefully setting the table
for two. I passed you the toast –
you sat there. I passed
you the paper – you hid
behind it.
Anger seemed more familiar.
I burned the toast, snatched
the paper and read the headlines myself.
But they mentioned your departure
and so I moved on to
Bargaining. What could I exchange
for you? The silence
after storms? My typing fingers?
Before I could decide, Depression
came puffing up, a poor relation
its suitcase tied together
with string. In the suitcase
were bandages for the eyes
and bottles of sleep. I slid
all the way down the stairs
feeling nothing.
And all the time Hope
flashed on and off

93

in defective neon.
Hope was a signpost pointing
straight in the air.
Hope was my uncle's middle name,
He died of it.
After a year I am still climbing,
though my feet slip
on your stone face.
The treeline
has long since disappeared;
green is a color
I have forgotten.
But now I see what I am climbing
towards: Acceptance
written in capital letters,
a special headline:
Acceptance.
Its name is in lights.
I struggle on,
waving and shouting.
Below, my whole life spreads its surf,
all the landscape I've ever known
or dreamed of. Below
a fish jumps: the pulse
in your neck.
Acceptance. I finally
Reach it.
But something is wrong.
Grief is a circular suitcase.
I have lost you.

Linda Pastan

After My Death

After I am dead
Say this at my funeral:

There was a man who exists no more.

That man died before his time
And his life's song was broken off halfway.
Oh, he had one more poem
And that poem has been lost
For ever.

He had a lyre,
And a vital, quivering soul.
The poet in him spoke,
Gave out all his heart's secrets,
His hand struck all its chords.
But there was one secret he kept hidden
Though his fingers danced everywhere,
One string stayed mute
And is still soundless.

But alas! All its days
That string trembled,
Trembled softly, softly quivered
For the poem that would free her,
Yearned and thirsted, grieved and wept,
As though pining for someone expected
Who does not come,
And the more he delays, she whimpers
With a soft, fine sound,
But he does not come,
And the agony is very great,
There was a man and he exists no more.
His life's song was broken off halfway.

He had one more poem
And that poem is lost,
For ever.

Chaim Nachman Bialik

The Choice

If we could hang all our sorrows on pegs and were allowed
to choose those we liked best, every one of us would take
back his own, for all the rest would seem even more difficult
to bear.

Martin Buber

For My Daughter on Her Twenty-First Birthday

When they laid you in the crook
of my arms like a bouquet and I looked
into your eyes, dark bits of evening sky,
I thought, *of course this is you,*
like a person who has never seen the sea
can recognize it instantly.

They pulled you from me like a cork
and all the love flowed out. I adored you
with the squandering passion of spring
that shoots green from every pore.

You dug me out like a well. You lit
the deadwood of my heart. You pinned me
to the earth with the points of stars.

I was sure that kind of love would be
enough. I thought I was your mother.
How could I have known that over and over

you would crack the sky like lightning,
illuminating all my fears, my weaknesses,
　　my sins.

Massive the burden this flesh
must learn to bear, like mules of love.

Ellen Bass

From Look There

The ceremony was modest.
A government clerk handed me
your final papers. You
who never graduated anything
were suddenly entitled to a lovely
death certificate
with the symbol of the state
as if you had mastered something
and fulfilled all the requirements.

She asked me if I wanted to update
(that's what she said)
father's death certificate.
Then she placed them side by side
like a pair of matching gravestones
and pressed the electric buzzer.

I went down to the street
walking
like a little girl
holding the hands
of paper parents
flapping in the wind.

Agi Mishol

The Seed of Eternal Life

We obsess too much about living longer, we think too little about elevating the life we have. How, in all conscience, can we demand a life after death if we have not invested our life with eternal quality?

If God has planted the seed of life everlasting in us, then eternity is a quality with which our life can be suffused. Heschel described eternity as 'not perpetual future but perpetual presence', adding that the *olam haba*, the world to come, was 'not only a hereafter but also a *herenow*'.

Editors, inspired by A. J. Heschel

In Mourning for Yekutiel

See the sun redden in the evening
As if she had put on a scarlet robe.
She strips the north and south of colour,
And the west she clothes in purple.
And the earth – she leaves it naked,
Cowering in the shadow of night.
The skies darken, dressed in black,
In mourning for Yekutiel.

Solomon ibn Gabirol

They Say 'Time Heals'

They say 'Time heals'
and 'He had a good life'
and 'He was over eighty, an old man after all'
and 'Lucky that he did not suffer so much'

And I do not reply
and the grief wells up inside,
and the pain tears through me
And I do not reply.

Seymour Freedman

As Propriety Demands

Mourn for a few days, as propriety demands, and then take
    comfort for your grief.
For grief may lead to death, and a sorrowful heart saps the
    strength …
Do not abandon yourself to grief; put it from you and
    think of your own end.
Never forget, there is no return; you cannot help him and
    can only injure yourself.
Remember that his fate will also be yours: 'Mine today and
    yours tomorrow.'
When the dead is at rest, let his memory rest too; take
    comfort as soon as he has breathed his last.

Ben Sira 38.17–23

What We Really Lose

What is it we really lose? His body is made of matter that
becomes other forms and other life. His heart is not lost.
His love doesn't disappear just because he died; it's with
me, our children, grandchildren and all who knew him. It
travels on to nurture other lives. As for his mind, I know
his thoughts intimately and can say what he would think in
almost every situation. The books he loved are all around
me, I have letters and diaries he wrote. His spirit continues

99

on its journey because the spirit never dies. What is it then that we really mourn? It is the presence of the person we love among us day by day. That is what we lose; but everything they have been travels on.

Jonathan Wittenberg

From Psalm 30

I exalt you, God, for you raised me up.
My God, my Protector,
I cried out to you and you healed me.
God, you brought up my soul from below,
You kept me alive, stopped me sinking into the grave.
Sing psalms to God, you who love God,
and give thanks
as you remember God's holy ways:
anger that lasts for a moment,
favour that lasts a lifetime.
Tears may linger at evening,
but in the morning comes joy.
you turned my mourning into dancing ...
so my soul sings your psalms,
silent no longer;
my God, my Protector,
I praise you for ever and ever.

Psalm 30.2–6, 12–13

10

Words of Comfort

Eternal God, help me to feel Your presence even when dark shadows fall upon me. When my own weakness and the storms of life hide You from my sight, help me to know that You have not deserted me. Uphold me with the comfort of Your love!

Siddur Lev Chadash

For thus says the Eternal One:
As a mother comforts her child, so will I comfort you.

Isaiah 66.13a

As a father has compassion on his children,
So You, Eternal God, have compassion on those who
    revere You.

Psalm 103.13

If We Choose Rightly

The intelligent heart does not deny reality. We must not forget the grief of yesterday, nor ignore the pain of today. But yesterday is past, it cannot tell us what tomorrow will bring. If there is goodness at the heart of life, then its power, like the power of evil, is real. Which shall prevail? Moment by moment, we choose between them. If we choose rightly, and often enough, the broken fragments of our world will be restored to wholeness.

For this, we need strength and help. We turn in hope, therefore, to a Power beyond us. God has many names, but God is One. God creates; God sustains; God loves; God inspires us with the hope that we can make ourselves one, as Adonai is One.

Chaim Stern

Death and Dying

One of the Torah-Masters taught:

The day Rabbi Akiva died, Rabbi Yehuda the Prince was
    born.
When Rabbi Yehuda the Prince died, Rav Yehuda was
    born.
When Rav Yehuda died, Rava was born.
When Rava died, Rav Ashi was born,
which indicates that no Righteous Person dies until a
    similar one is created,
as the Biblical verse shows,
'The sun rises, and the sun sets.' (Ecclesiastes 1.5)

Talmud Kiddushin 72b

Coronary Connections

Who can rant against science and technology, as if they stood in opposition to faith and religion? Are these marvellously contrived machines not instruments of divinity? Blessed is the human mind who can put together fragmented parts, make strong fragile organs, circumvent dead parts, and connect life with life. Look where for miracles? We carry them in our flesh and blood.

Blessed is the curative wisdom of the body.

We pray wrong. To pray is not to pay off your debt to some celestial creditor. It is not some unnatural act of piety. To pray is to notice, to pay attention, to overcome the apathy of entitlement. I look with new eyes at the opening prayers of our daily service, bursting with gratitude for opening the eyes of the blind, for raising up those bowed down, for guiding the step, for strengthening the weary.

I am not the only one who has been afflicted by illness, and not the only one frightened by death and by life, but I now have a knowledge different from that drawn from texts. Knowledge by acquaintance is different from knowledge by description. It is one thing to read about it or to hear about it from another, and something else to offer testimony out of your own flesh. I have come out of this, not with revelations, but with the testimony of old truths renewed.

For Judaism, life is holy – not life in another time or another place, not life in heaven among angelic forms – but this one here and now with all its human agonies and frustrations. There is basic to Judaism an intense thirst for life ...

Life is holy and life is plural – as it is grammatically plural in the Hebrew term *chayim*. What a conceit to think of myself as a self-sufficient biosystem, a portable set of plumbing, a self bounded by my outer skin. What a deceit is played upon us by the false intimacy of 'me' or 'I'. There is no solitary life. There is no I without Thou, no 'me' without 'us'. For our life, we are profoundly dependent upon each other.

Harold M. Schulweis

God Gives Us Strength

The God I believe in does not send us the problem; He gives us the strength to cope with the problem.

Where do you get the strength to go on, when you have used up all of your strength? Where do you turn for patience when you have run out of patience, when you have been more patient for more years than anyone should be asked to be, and the end is nowhere in sight? I believe that God gives us strength and patience and hope, renewing our spiritual resources when they run dry. How else do sick people manage to find more strength and more good humour over the course of prolonged illness than any one person could possibly have, unless God was constantly replenishing their souls? How else do widows find the courage to pick up the pieces of their lives and go out to face the world alone, when on the day of their husband's funeral, they did not have that courage? How else do the parents of a retarded or brain-damaged youngster wake up every morning and turn again to their responsibilities, unless they are able to lean on God when they grow weak?

Harold S. Kushner

I Am Older Now: A Yahrzeit Candle Lit at Home

The *yahrzeit* candle is different,
announcing neither Sabbath nor festival.
No benediction recited
No song sung
No psalm mandated.

Before this unlit candle
without a quorum, I stand
unstruck match in my hand.

It is less distant now,
the remembrance ritual of parents deceased.
I am older now,
closer to their age than before.
I am older now,
their aches in my body
their white hairs beneath my shaved skin
their wrinkles creased into my face.

It is less distant now
this ritual
once made me think of them
Now makes me think of me.

Once it recalled relationships to them
Now I ponder my children's relationship to me.
Once I wondered what to remember of them
Now I ask what my children remember of me
what smile, what grimace
What stories they will tell their children of me.

It is less distant now.
How will I be remembered
How will I be mourned

Will they come to the synagogue
light a candle
recite the *Kaddish*?
It is less distant now.
Once *yahrzeit* was about parents deceased,
Now it is of children alive.
Once it was about a distant past,
Now it is about tomorrow.

Harold M. Schulweis

Consolation

There are sorrows whose roots the sympathy of best friends cannot reach. There are burdens so heavy that no human being can help to lift or bear them. There are some whose wounds are too raw even for a friendly touch. What must it mean to such people to know and to feel that One greater than humanity is there with a sympathy silent but how tender! With a balm unseen but how healing. One to whom a heart can pour out its torrents of bitterness without words. A Friend with the tenderness of a mother, with a healing knowledge, and power how healing.

Israel I. Mattuck (attrib.)

The Soul's Survival

Death cannot be and is not the end of life. Man transcends death in many altogether naturalistic fashions. He may be immortal biologically, through his children, in thought through the survival of his memory; in influence, by virtue of the continuance of his personality as a force among those who come after him, and, ideally, through identification with the timeless things of the spirit.

When Judaism speaks of immortality it has in mind all of these. But its primary meaning is that man contains something independent of the flesh and surviving it; his consciousness and moral capacity; his essential personality; a soul.

Milton Steinberg

Life on Earth

As Jacob prepared to die he demanded that his son Joseph bury his remains in the family burial site of Machpelah, rather than in Egypt. We may wonder why he wished to put his sons to all the trouble of bearing his body from Egypt to a Canaanite tomb? Perhaps he chose this course because he witnessed the Egyptian fixation with death, the enormous resources that went into creating lavish tombs for a comfortable afterlife. This is not the Jewish way, indeed it is contrary to the Jewish spirit. We show respect and honour to the dead, but we give our maximum effort to the living. We may hope for immortality, but it is life on earth which is our principal focus.

Editors, inspired by Solomon B. Freehof

Stronger than Death

According to Rabbi Yehudah; ten strong things were created in the world: rock is strong, but iron cleaves it; iron is strong, but fire melts it; fire is strong, but water quenches it; water is strong but clouds bear it away; clouds are strong, but wind drives them; winds are strong, but man resists them; man is strong but fear casts him down; fear is strong but wine casts it out; wine is strong but sleep dissolves it; sleep is strong but

death is stronger; and loving kindness is stronger yet, for it
survives death.

Talmud Baba Batra 10a

Psalm 90

A Prayer of Moses, the man of God

Lord, you have been our dwelling-place
   in all generations.
Before the mountains were brought forth,
   or ever you had formed the earth and the world,
   from everlasting to everlasting you are God.

You turn us back to dust, and say, 'Turn back you mortals.'
For a thousand years in your sight are like yesterday when
   it is past,
   or like a watch in the night.

You sweep them away, they are like a dream,
   like grass that is renewed in the morning;
in the morning it flourishes and is renewed;
   in the evening it fades and withers.

For all our days pass away under your wrath;
   our years come to an end like a sigh.
The days of our life are seventy years,
   or perhaps eighty, if we are strong;
even then their span is only toil and trouble;
   they are soon gone, and we fly away.

Who considers the power of your anger?
Your wrath is as great as the fear that is due to you.
So teach us to count our days that we may gain a wise
   heart.

Turn, O Lord! How long?
  Have compassion on your servants!
Satisfy us in the morning with your steadfast love,
  so that we may rejoice and be glad all our days.
Make us glad for as many days as you have afflicted us,
  and for as many years as we have seen evil.
Let your work be manifest to your servants,
  and your glorious power to their children.
Let the favour of the Lord our God be upon us
  and prosper for us the work of our hands –
O prosper the work of our hands!

(NRSV)

A Child's Comfort

When my father died over two decades ago, I cried a lot. My children were of enormous comfort. I remember the way my daughter held me and the way my oldest son took a shovel at the graveside and helped my brother and me cover the coffin with earth.

On the morning of the funeral, my then eleven-year-old son came and sat in my lap to console me. We cried and we hugged and sat in silence. And then, in a moment of great insight, the little one burst out crying again and through the tears said, 'The hardest part, Daddy, is knowing that someday I'll have to do this for you.'

'I only hope you will have such a wonderful son to help you, the way you are helping me!' I said. 'Come, it is time to go to the cemetery.'

Lawrence Kushner

Fear Not Death

Fear not death; we are destined to die. We share it with all who ever lived, with all who ever will be. Bewail the dead, hide not your grief, do not restrain your mourning. But remember that continuing sorrow is worse than death. When the dead are at rest, let their memory rest, and be consoled when the soul departs.

Death is better than a life of pain, and eternal rest than constant sickness.

Seek not to understand what is too difficult for you, search not for what is hidden from you. Be not over-occupied with what is beyond you, for you have been shown more than you can understand.

As a drop of water in the sea, as a grain of sand on the shore are man's few days in eternity. The good things in life last for limited days, but a good name endures for ever.

after Ben Sira

Conclusion of Shiv'ah

At the conclusion of shiv'ah, the following may be said.

God is our refuge, and our strength; He is always our help in adversity. Therefore, even though the earth should change, we shall not fear. In all misfortune, He is our stronghold. Sorrow has been our daily bread, and tears of grief have been our drink. May the God of compassion, the light in our midst, lead us now to life. He will heal us, time after time. He calls our life away from the grave, surrounds us with goodness and tender love. May He heal our wounds, and may He heal the wounds of all the people of Israel. And let us say: Amen.

As a mother comforts her children, so shall I comfort you, says the Lord. The Lord heals the broken-hearted; He binds up their wounds. The Lord will be your enduring light, and the days of your mourning will come to an end.

Almighty God, Master of mercy, Healer of the broken-hearted, let neither death nor sorrow have dominion over us. Grant us strength as we mourn the loss of ....
May we always cherish what is imperishable in the life of .... Bless our family with love and with peace, that we may serve You with all our heart. May the memory of .... inspire us to deeds of lovingkindness. And let us say: Amen.

The Bond of Life

Psalm 131

My heart is not proud, O God, and my eyes are not
   haughty;
On things beyond my scope no more I brood.
But I have calmed and quieted my soul, like a child at its
   mother's breast;
My soul is like a comforted child.
O Israel, trust in the Eternal One, now and for ever.

Siddur Lev Chadash

Legacy

A Time for Everything

There is a time for everything.
A time for all things under heaven:
A time to be born and a time to die,
A time to plant and a time to uproot,
A time to slay and a time to heal,
A time to tear down and a time to build,
A time to weep and a time to laugh,
A time to wail and a time to dance,
A time to scatter and a time to gather,
A time to embrace and a time to shun embraces,
A time to seek and a time to lose,
A time to keep and a time to discard,
A time to tear and a time to sew,

A time for silence and a time for speech,
A time for love and a time for hate,
A time for war and a time for peace.

A time to be born and a time to die.

Ecclesiastes 3.1–8, 2

Give Me the Vision

Shall I cry out in anger, O God,
Because Your gifts are mine but for a while?
Shall I be ungrateful for the moments of laughter,
The seasons of joy, the days of gladness and festivity,
When tears cloud my eyes and darken the world
And my heart is heavy within me?
Shall I blot from mind the love
I have known and in which I have rejoiced
When a fate beyond my understanding takes from me
Friends and kin whom I have cherished, and leaves me
Bereft of shining presences that have lit my way
Through years of companionship and affection?
Give me the vision, O God, to see and feel
That imbedded deep in each of Your gifts
Is a core of eternity, undiminished and bright
that survives the dread hours
of affliction and misery.
Those I have loved, though now beyond my view,
Have given form and quality to my being.
They have led me into the wide universe
I continue to inhabit, and their presence
Is more vital to me than their absence.

What You give, O Lord,
You do not take away.
And bounties once granted
Shed their radiance evermore.

Morris Adler

When Bad Things Happen to Good People

The facts of life and death are neutral. We, by our responses, give suffering either a positive or a negative meaning. Illnesses, accidents, human tragedies kill people. But they do not necessarily kill life or faith. If the death and suffering of someone we love makes us bitter, jealous, against all religion, and incapable of happiness, *we* turn the person who died into one of the 'devil's martyrs'. If suffering and death in someone close to us brings us to explore the limits of our capacity for strength and love and cheerfulness, if it leads us to discover sources of consolation we never knew before, then we make the person into a witness for the affirmation of life rather than its rejection.

In the final analysis, the question of why bad things happen to good people translates itself into some very different questions, no longer asking why something happened, but asking how we will respond, what we intend to do now that it has happened.

Harold S. Kushner

The Dead Go On Living

These things I know:
how the living go on living
and how the dead go on living
with them

so that in a forest
even a dead tree casts a shadow
and the leaves fall one by one

and the branches break in the wind
and the bark peels off slowly
and the trunk cracks
and the rain seeps in through the cracks
and the trunk falls to the ground
and the moss covers it
and in the spring the rabbits find it

and build their nest
inside the dead tree
so that nothing is wasted in nature
or in love.

Laura Gilpin

When Our World is Not Complete

It is hard to sing of oneness when our world is not complete,
when those who once brought wholeness to our life have
    gone,
and naught but memory can fill the emptiness their passing
    leaves behind.

But memory can tell us only what we were, in company
    with those we loved;

it cannot help us find what each of us, alone, must now
  become.
Yet no one is really alone:
those who live no more, echo still within our thoughts and
  words,
and what they did is part of what we have become.

We do best homage to our dead when we live our lives
  more fully,
even in the shadow of our loss.
For each of our lives is worth the life of the whole world;
in each one is the breath of the Ultimate One.
In affirming the One, we affirm the words of each one
whose life, now ended, brought us closer to the Source of
  life,
in whose unity no one is alone and every life finds purpose.

Richard N. Levy

Vanished Stars

There are stars up above,
so far away we only see their light
long, long after the star itself is gone.

And so it is with people that we loved –
their memories keep shining ever brightly
though their time with us is done.
But the stars that light up the darkest night,
these are the lights that guide us.
As we live our days, these are the ways we remember.

Hannah Senesh

To Love and Lose

It is a fearful thing to love
what death can touch.

A fearful thing to love,
hope, dream: to be –
to be, and oh! to lose.

A thing for fools this, and
a holy thing,
a holy thing to love.

For
your life has lived in me,
your laugh once lifted me,
your word was gift to me.

To remember this brings a painful joy.
'Tis a human thing, love,
a holy thing,
to love
what death has touched.

Chaim Stern

A Prayer

In Nature's ebb and flow, God's eternal law abides.
When tears dim our vision or grief clouds our understanding,
we often lose sight of God's eternal plan.
Yet we know that growth and decay, life and death,
all reveal a divine purpose.
God who is our support in the struggles of life, is also our
    hope in death.
We have set God before us and shall not despair.

In God's hands are the souls of all the living and the spirits
of all flesh.
Under God's protection we abide, and by God's love are
we comforted.
O Life of our life, Soul of our soul, cause Your light to
shine into our hearts,
and fill our spirits with abiding trust in You.

Union Prayer Book

Life is a Candle

The light of life is a finite flame.
Like the Shabbat candles,
life is kindled, it burns, it glows,
it is radiant with warmth and beauty.
But soon it fades, its substance is consumed,
and it is no more.

In light we see;
in light we are seen.
The flames dance
and our life burns down and gutters.
There is an end to the flames.
We see no more
and are no more seen,
yet we do not despair,
for we are more than a memory
slowly fading into the darkness.
With our lives we give life.
Something of us can never die:
we move in the eternal cycle
of darkness and death,
of light and life.

Chaim Stern

The Ethical Will

What is the true legacy I can leave my own children?
It is not stocks and bonds and notes and
precious stones. It is not even such wisdom as I may have
  accumulated
in my life. For what is man and what is life? I have lived
and I will die, but the deepest mysteries of life will no
  doubt
be as unclear to me at the end as at
the beginning.

Each of us is but a puff of smoke in eternity.
What is immortal about us is that we are part of
an undying Jewish people. The wisdom which has
been distilled in 3,000 years of unique history
is the greatest legacy a Jew can leave his children.
For it is not economic wealth, but moral and
spiritual treasure which I can pass on to my
children as did my ancestors through one hundred
and twelve generations, stretching back to the
mists of Sinai. What I owe them is a chance
to grasp a faith to live by.

Albert Vorspan

A Good Jew

Before he died Rabbi Shelomo Hayyim said to his son:
    You are not to think that your father was a 'Tzaddik', or
    a 'rebbe' or a 'good Jew'. But all the same I haven't been
    a hypocrite, I did try to be a good Jew.

Martin Buber

The Essential Me

My religious experience offers me the assurance that, though my body will one day give out, the essential Me will live on, and if I am concerned with immortality of that sort, I should pay at least as much attention to my soul, my non-physical self, as I do my weight and my blood pressure. God cannot redeem me from death, no matter how good a person I am, but He redeems me from the fear of death so that I don't have to clutch frantically at this life as if it were all there is. He lights my path through the 'valley of the shadow of death' by assuring me that the words I have written and spoken, the hearts I have touched, the hands I have reached out to, the child I will leave behind, will gain me all the immortality I need. More than that, I am assured that even when the last person who ever knew me dies, and the last copy of my book has been removed from the library shelf, the essential me, the non-physical me, will still live on in the mind of God, where no act of goodness or kindness is ever forgotten.

Harold S. Kushner

Long Gone

Both my grandmas came from far away
on the difficult journey alone with their children
to this strange and terrifying country.
They had the courage to do that
but only enough strength
to get here, raise their kids, and die.
I myself have stood on the shore of the Caspian Sea
and know how far away far can be
and how far this America was from their homes,

from the life they yearned back to.
But they lived here uprooted the rest of their lives.

You died, dear ones, not knowing
that your grandson loved you
and would remember you one day when he was nearly fifty
and need you, and wish, my angels, you were there.
Eat, eat, *tottele*, you would say
if you saw me crying now.
For you were so humble
you could not believe you had anything else to offer.
And maybe eating is life's one reliable consolation
after the disappointment men turned out to be
and the anguish of their children's lives.

You are long gone, my grandmas.
People are so fragile
and it is impossible to protect our dear ones
from the terrible things that happen to them ...

I know when I think of you, my grandmas,
that you are my connection with my ancestors
whom I have somehow lost.
How did the energy line get broken?
When you crossed the sea?
When I grew up an American and so different from my
    father
but as he wanted me to be,
not speaking his heart's language or knowing the
    synagogue?
So I go on crying all my life, for you, for me, for my ma,
afraid of the dark, afraid of the man who will come get me,
and most of all afraid of the power in me
that life has not used.

I won't ever forget you again.
Both of you are with me now, and through you, all my
    people.
I have the strength of all of you,
and your sorrow, and your defeat.

Thanks to you, I know who I am.

Edward Field

Missing Parents

In many houses
all at once
I see my mother and father
and they are young
as they walk in.
Why should my
tears come, to see them laughing?

That they cannot
see me
is of no matter:
I was once
their dream:
now
they are mine.

Anon

From Psalm 15

Eternal God:
Who may abide in Your house?
Who may dwell in Your holy mountain?

Those who are upright; who do justly;
all whose hearts are true.
Who do not slander others,
nor wrong them,
nor bring shame upon their kin.
Who give their word and, come what may, do not retract.
Who do not exploit others,
who never take bribes.
Those who live in this way shall never be shaken.

Psalm 15.1–3, 5–6

From Psalm 63

O God, you are my God, I seek you,
   my soul thirsts for you;
my flesh faints for you,
   as in a dry and weary land where there is no water.
So I have looked upon you in the sanctuary,
   beholding your power and glory.
Because your steadfast love is better than life,
   my lips will praise you.
So I will bless you as long as I live;
   I will lift up my hands and call on your name.

My soul is satisfied as with a rich feast,
   and my mouth praises you with joyful lips
when I think of you on my bed,
   and meditate on you in the watches of the night;
for you have been my help,
   and in the shadow of your wings I sing for joy.
My soul clings to you;
   Your right hand upholds me.

Psalm 63.1–9

12

Gratitude

An Alternative Psalm IV

O Lord,
You are a consolation to Your creatures,
for in moments of forgetting,
we but call to mind Your care,
and we are comforted.
When we hope no more,
a pattern in the snow
reminds us of Your lovingkindness.
Your dawns give us confidence,
and sleep is a friend.
Our sorrows dissipate
in the presence of an infant's smile,
and old men's words revive our will-to-wish.
Your hints are everywhere,
Your signals in the most remote of places.

You are here,
and we fail words to say,
'*Mah Tov!*'
How good our breath,
our rushing energies,
our silences of love.

Danny Siegel

From Psalm 108

My heart is steadfast, O God, my heart is steadfast;
    I will sing and make melody. Awake, my soul!
Awake, O harp and lyre!
    I will awake the dawn.
I will give thanks to you, O Lord, among the peoples,
    and I will sing praises to You among the nations.
For Your steadfast love is higher than the heavens,
    and Your faithfulness reaches to the clouds.

Psalm 108.2–4

What is Good Cannot Perish

You have called me into life, setting me in the midst of
purposes I cannot measure or understand. Yet I thank You
for the good I know, for the life I have, and for the gifts that
– in sickness and in health – have been my daily portion:
the beauty of earth and sky, the visions that have stirred me
from my ease and quickened my endeavours, the demands
of truth and justice that move me to acts of goodness, and
the contemplation of Your eternal presence, which fills me
with hope that what is good and lovely cannot perish. For
all this, I give thanks.

Chaim Stern

The Shelter of God's Peace

Grant, Eternal God, that we may lie down in peace, and let us rise up to life renewed. Spread over us the shelter of Your peace; guide us with Your wise counsel and for Your Name's sake, be our help. Shield us from sickness and war, famine and distress, and keep us from wrongdoing. Shelter us in the shadow of Your wings, for You are our Guardian and Deliverer, a gracious and merciful God. Guard our going out and our coming in, that, now and always, we may have life and peace. We praise You, O God: may Your sheltering peace descend on us and all who dwell on earth

Siddur Lev Chadash

The End is a Beginning

It's always impressed me that Judaism mandates that goodbyes be said with a certain amount of hope. We end Shabbat with havdalah, a beautiful ceremony concluded by extinguishing a twisted candle in sweet wine and singing a song asking for a week of peace and a time of redemption for humankind. Seders end with the promise 'Next year in Jerusalem'. On Simchat Torah, we conclude the reading of the Torah by rolling back to its beginning. Funerals end with Kaddish, a prayer not about death but about the generous gift of life and God's goodness. At the completion of shiva, the rabbi often takes the mourners out of their home for a brief stroll that enacts literally what is meant symbolically – walking them back into life. Somehow Jews trust that every ending is also a beginning, that the broken hearted will again feel loved, and the sun will rise no matter how long or dark the night.

Steven Z. Leder

Annual Miracle

Now in the winter we despair of warmth.
Earth, air and waters are alike frozen.

We tend the little fires in our homes
And shivering, we long for sun and spring.

Everywhere is the white hand of death;
The trees are skeletons, the birds are gone.

And yet we know life is underground,
Beneath the snow, in roots of trees and plants.

We know fish swim in ice-locked waters
And a cocoon folded in a dried leaf holds a butterfly.

Here in the winter, as if to chide our unbelief,
God gives us this annual miracle:

This icy death is neither fatal nor forever,
For God is a lover of life.

Ruth F. Brin

From Psalm 116

I love the Eternal One, who hears my supplications,
whose ear is turned to me whenever I call.
The bonds of death encompassed me, the torments
of Sheol found me out;
I met trouble and sorrow, and cried out to the Eternal One:
'O God, save me!'
God is gracious and just, our God is compassionate.
The Eternal One protects the simple, I was brought low
   and God saved me.
Be calm again, my soul, for God has been good to you.

You have saved my soul from death, my eyes from tears,
my feet from stumbling.
I shall walk before God in the land of the living.
I cling to my faith even when I cry out in affliction,
rashly saying that all people are false.
How can I show my gratitude, O God, for all Your
kindnesses?
I shall lift up the cup of salvation and call out Your name
in praise.
I shall bring You my offering of thanks, and call upon
Your name.

Psalm 116.1–13, 17

13

Memory

Some of us recall the image of beloved parents who, even before we were born, had prepared a secure home for us in which we could find shelter during our years of helplessness and dependence, who watched over us with solicitous care, nursed us, guided us, and taught us to know You, to trust You as our Divine Parent and to commit ourselves to Your law of righteousness. Some of us call to mind a wife or a husband with whom we were so united by the sacred covenant of marriage that we became one flesh and one spirit. Some of us remember brothers and sisters, who grew up together with us, sharing in the play of childhood, in the youthful adventure of exploring life's possibilities, bound to us by a common heritage of family tradition and a faithful comradeship that enhanced the joys and mitigated the sorrows of life through the divine power of love. Some of us cannot forget children, entrusted for a while to our care but called away by death before they had time even to reach the years of maturity and fulfilment, to whom we gave our loving care and from whom we received that trust and confidence which enriched our lives. All of us recall some beloved persons whose friendship, affection and devotion elicited the best in us, and whose visible presence will never return to cheer, encourage or inspire us.

Ronald Aigen

What is Memory?

Where does yesterday go?
What happens to the days which have passed?
Are they consumed as objects which are destroyed by fire,
Leaving only ashes behind?
Or is there perhaps some indestructible quality
Which can save the past from annihilation?
The answer lies not in the days themselves,
But rather in us.
It rests within our power to save the yesterdays
And the means for achieving this is memory.
What is memory?
It is the God-given gift
of being able to behold the
golden days of the sunset
which went before
while standing in the ensuing gloom.
It is the ability to hear the sweet melody
After the instruments have ceased playing.
What is memory?
It is the ability to feel the zeal and spirit of youth
In the midst of the disillusionments of the later life.
It is the ability to dance in the heart
When the legs can no longer keep up with the music.

What is memory?
It is the gazing at the bride beneath the canopy
and remembering the infant in the crib.
It is playing with the grandchildren
and seeing their parents.
It is celebrating a boy's Bar Mitzvah
and simultaneously attending the Bris.
What is memory?
It is experiencing today the heartache of yesterday.
It is the sorrow in the present for an agony of the past.
It is a conversation with someone who can no longer speak.
And the sight of a smile on a face no longer here.
What is memory?
It is all that is left to us
From the burnt-out hopes and strivings,
as well as the pain and sorrow, of the past.
What is memory?
It is that in which, above all else,
is to be found the source of our immortality.

Harry Halpern

Heirloom

My father bequeathed in me no wide estates;
No keys and ledgers were my heritage;
Only some holy books with *yahrzeit* dates
Writ mournfully upon a blank front page –

Books of the Baal Shem Tov, and of his wonders,
Pamphlets upon the devil and his crew;
Prayers against road demons, witches, thunders;
And sundry other tomes for a good Jew.

Beautiful: though no pictures on them, save
The Scorpion crawling on a printed track;
The Virgin floating on a scriptural wave,
Square letters twinkling in the Zodiac.

The snuff left on this title page, now brown and old,
The tallow stains of midnight liturgy –
These are my coat of arms, and these unfold
My noble lineage, my proud ancestry!

And my tears, too, have stained this heirloomed ground,
When reading in these treatises some weird
Miracle, I turned a leaf and found
A white hair fallen from my father's beard.

A. M. Klein

Letting Go

One wears his mind out in study, and yet has more mind
with which to study. One gives away his heart in love, and
yet has more heart to give away. One perishes out of pity
for a suffering world, and is the stronger therefore. So, too,
it is possible at one and the same time to hold on to life and
let it go ...

Milton Steinberg

Dad

Your old hat hurts me, and those black
    fat raisins you liked to press into
my palm from your soft heavy hand.
    I see you staggering back up the path
with sacks of potatoes from some local farm,
    fresh eggs, flowers. Every day I grieve

for your great heart broken and you gone.
    You loved to watch the trees. This year
you did not see their Spring.
    The sky was freezing over the fen
as on that somewhere secretly appointed day
    you beached: cold, white-faced, shivering.

What happened, old bull, my loyal
    hoarse-voiced warrior? The hammer
blow that stopped you in your track
    and brought you to a hospital monitor
could not destroy your courage
    to the end you were
uncowed and unconcerned with pleasing anyone.

I think of you now as once again safely
    at my mother's side, the earth as
chosen as a bed, and feel most sorrow for
    all that was gentle in
my childhood buried there
    already forfeit, now forever lost.

Elaine Feinstein

Mother and Father

My mother was a prophet and didn't know it.
Not like Miriam the prophetess dancing with cymbals and
    tambourines,
not like Deborah who sat under the palm tree and judged
    the people,
not like Hulda who foretold the future,
but my own private prophet, silent and stubborn.
I am obliged to fulfil everything she said
and I'm running out of lifetime.

My mother was a prophet when she taught me
the do's and don'ts of everyday, paper verses
for one-time use: You'll be sorry,
you'll get exhausted, that will do you good, you'll feel
like a new person, you'll really love it, you
won't be able, you won't like that, you'll never manage
to close it, I knew you wouldn't remember, wouldn't
forget give take rest, yes you can you can.
And when my mother died, all her little predictions came
    together
in one big prophecy that will last
until the vision of the end of days.

My father was God and didn't know it. He gave me
the Ten Commandments not in thunder and not in anger,
not in fire and not in a cloud, but gently
and with love. He added caresses and tender words,
'would you' and 'please'. And chanted 'remember' and
    'keep'
with the same tune, and pleaded and wept quietly
between one commandment and the next. Thou shalt not
take the name of thy Lord in vain, shalt not take, not in
    vain,
please don't bear false witness against your neighbour.
And he hugged me tight and whispered in my ear,
Thou shalt not steal, shalt not commit adultery, shalt not
    kill.
And he lay the palms of his wide-open hands on my head
with the Yom Kippur blessing: Honour, love, that thy days
may be long upon this earth. And the voice of my father –
white as his hair. Then he turned his face to me one last
    time,
as on the day he died in my arms, and said, I would like to
    add

two more commandments:
the Eleventh Commandment, 'Thou shalt not change',
and the Twelfth Commandment, 'Thou shalt change. You
  will change.'
Thus he spoke my father and he turned and walked away
and disappeared into his strange distances.

Yehuda Amichai

She was Beautiful

My mother's mother died in the spring of her days.
And her daughter did not remember her face.
Her portrait, engraved upon my grandfather's heart,
was erased from the world of images after his death.

Only her mirror remained in the home, sunken with age
  into the silver frame.
And I, her pale granddaughter, who does not resemble her,
look into it today as into a pool which conceals its
  treasures beneath the waters.

Very deep, behind my face, I see a young woman
pink-cheeked, smiling and a wig on her head.
She puts an elongated earring on her earlobe, threading it
through a tiny hole in the dainty flesh of her ear.

Very deep behind my face,
the bright goldness of her eyes sends out rays,
and the mirror carries on the tradition of the family:
that she was very beautiful.

Leah Goldberg

You Live Within Me

I used to be part of you
belong to you
the extension of your being
but now
you live within me
are the spark
of my consciousness

I say Kaddish for you
with you
as you
sing your melodies
speak your words
hearing your voice in mine
and my eyes
too green
have somehow started to reflect
the blue of yours

I used to be part of you
protected by your presence
by your light
but now
the time is mine
and alone
I must be more than myself:
your child
has become your heir
has become you.

Menachem Rosensaft

Anniversary

Everywhere I look I see you.
April again. The coffee sitting too long
in its white cup leaves a ring the colour of your straw hat,
the one you wore in the garden. In forsythia, I see you.
The small diamond chip in a stranger's ear.
On the bus I see you, and in galleries and cafes.
Your red coat. I see you young and I see you old.
Imagine, I see you old! Illumined by white hair, you are
drinking juice. I see you in paintbrushes and water towers.
On evening walks, in the broken sky
between buildings, I piece you
together.
It is Passover again.
I see you at the *seder*, your pink and white robe,
in sweet apples and salt water, in the blunt, bitter root.
Tell me, exactly when is the moment
of passing?

I travel to the desert, and there you are –
the low airport buildings are yours; the sudden mountains,
yours. I see you in the clear light, the thin air,
the fifty shades of green beside the road. At midday,
the rutted hills are your hands. We drive
and I see them all day long.

I see you as you were, and as you never were.
In charcoal and in flesh, with the unrelenting mind
of Spring, I see you. The petal of the crocus
that clings to my finger, the purple capillaries
sprouting in my leg. You are the pavement under my feet,
the bucket of daffodils the grocer moves
to the front window.

Judy Katz

In the Jerusalem Hills

All the things
outside love
come to me now:
this landscape with its old man's understanding
begging to live
one more year, one more year,
one generation more, one more eternity.

To bring forth thorns endlessly,
to rock dead stones
like children in their cradles
before they sleep.
To silence ancient memories,
one more, one more,
one more.

How strong the lust for life
in those about to die.
How terrible the longing
and how vain:
to live, to live
one more year, one more year,
one generation more,
one more eternity.

Leah Goldberg

The Famous

Let us now praise famous men,
And our fathers that begat us.
The Lord manifested in them great glory,
Even his mighty power from the beginning.

Giving counsel by their understanding,
Such as have brought tidings in prophecies:
Leaders of the people by their counsels,
And by their understanding, men of learning for the people
Wise were their words in their instruction.
All these were honoured in their generations,
And were a glory in their days.
There be of them that have left a name behind them,
To declare their praises.
And some there be, which have no memorial;
Who are perished as though they had not been,
And are become as though they had not been born;
And their children after them.
But these were men of mercy,
Whose righteous deeds have not been forgotten.
Their seed shall remain for ever,
And their glory shall not be blotted out.
Peoples will declare their wisdom,
And the congregation telleth out their praise.

Ben Sira 44.1–10. 13–14

Remember Something

Try to remember some details. Remember the clothing
of the one you love
so that on the day of loss you'll be able to say: last seen
wearing such-and-such, brown jacket, white hat.
Try to remember some details. For they have no face
and their soul is hidden and their crying
is the same as their laughter,
and their silence and their shouting rise to one height
and their body temperature is between 98 and 104 degrees
and they have no life outside this narrow space

and they have no graven image, no likeness, no memory
and they have paper cups on the day of their rejoicing
and paper plates that are used once only.

Try to remember some details. For the world
is filled with people who were torn from their sleep
with no one to mend the tear,
and unlike wild beasts they live
each in his lonely hiding place and they die
together on battlefields
and in hospitals.
And the earth will swallow all of them,
good and evil together, like the followers of Korach,
all of them in their rebellion against death,
their mouths open till the last moment,
praising and cursing in a single
howl. Try, try,
to remember some details.

Yehuda Amichai

Yahrtzeit Candle

The candle burned through her memorial day.
Then the room grew dark when, fastened to its anchorage,
the wick drank in the last of melted wax,
and, after day-long hours of fragile flame,
consumed itself in quiet death.
As once before, when she took leave of life,
her tired flame consumed,
so now, once more, she died.

MEMORY

Do the valiant die but once? Not so.
The *eshet chayil's* passion was for life.
But life, which feeds the flame, can melt away,
until, at last, there is no more,
and all is gone – wick, flame, and light,
and only dark remains.
And so we die.
and in the *Yahrtzeit* candle die again.

Efraim M. Rosenzweig

14

Coda 2: Painful Memories

A Yizkor Meditation in Memory of a Parent Who was Hurtful

Dear God,

You know my heart. Indeed, You know me better than I know myself, so I turn to You before I rise for Kaddish.

My emotions swirl as I say this prayer. The parent I remember was not kind to me. His/her death left me with a legacy of unhealed wounds, of anger and of dismay that a parent could hurt a child as I was hurt.

I do not want to pretend to love, or to grief that I do not feel, but I do want to do what is right as a Jew and as a child.

Help me, O God, to subdue my bitter emotions that do me no good, and to find that place in myself where happier memories may lie hidden, and where grief for all that could have been, all that should have been, may be calmed by forgiveness, or at least soothed by the passage of time.

I pray that You, who raise up slaves to freedom, will liberate me from the oppression of my hurt and anger, and that You will lead me from this desert to Your holy place.

Robert Saks

My Mother

My mother complained that she never had her way.
It was simply: do as I say, freedom of choice is
an ungrateful luxury for a child.
And she never spoke of her mother.

Her bitterness grew with my years
and the shed and unshed tears walled
a great sadness that I could not penetrate
her sadness.

When she lay dying I was the pagan who promised
that her religious beliefs would not be violated,
that her burial would not be violated.
The plain pine box would be her final bed
and the rituals would be honoured. She would not believe
   me.

It was the day of the Sabbath Eve when she died.
And I called my son to say I need you now.
She was buried before sundown
And Gideon came for all the cousins.

And the rabbi said she was greatly blessed
to be buried on the day of death.

Before sundown
before the Sabbath Eve
was close to holiness.

And my grandson, my son, helped wheel
and put the pine box into the hearse – a ritual again
now doubly blessed, said the rabbi – ensuring her eternal
peace in heaven. My son with his choice of action
ensured her rest.

We put a stone on her grave and arranged for perennial care
so green plants could grow on her bitterness.
Beyond her greatest dreams.

I don't visit where she lies buried.
I have nothing to say to her.

I am afraid
that her earth will move.

Kalie Golden

Tattered Kaddish

Taurean reaper of the wild apple field
messenger from earthmire gleaming
transcripts of fog
in the nineteenth year and the eleventh month
speak your tattered Kaddish for all suicides:

Praise to life though it crumbled in like a tunnel
on ones we knew and loved

  Praise to life though its windows blew shut
  on the breathing-room of ones we knew and loved

CODA 2: PAINFUL MEMORIES

Praise to life though ones we knew and loved
loved it badly, too well, and not enough

    Praise to life though it tightened like a knot
    on the hearts of ones we thought we knew loved us

Praise to life giving room and reason
to ones we knew and loved who felt unpraisable

    Praise to them, how they loved it, when they could.

Adrienne Rich

15

Immortality and Life After Death

'Where Do People Go When They Die?'

The first and most honest answer to this question is that we don't know; nobody knows. No one who ever died has been able to tell those left behind what happened to him.

In fact, telling the living what happened in death would be impossible, because when people die they no longer see or feel or know anything. They don't feel uncomfortable about being put in a coffin or buried. They can't hear what we say about them. What *does* happen to them? The body of a dead person is put into the ground very respectfully, in a special place called a cemetery.

When he was alive, the person was more than a body. He was also what we call a soul, a personality. He was good at certain things; he cared about certain things and certain people. Things happened to him and he remembered them. All this made up his soul, the part of him that wasn't his body, that let him be him and nobody else. The question of what happens to a soul is a very hard one to answer, because a soul isn't a thing, a physical object which has to be in one place or another. A soul is a little bit like God – not an object, but a way of thinking and feeling, of making certain things happen.

Asking, 'Where does the soul go when a man dies?' is a little like asking 'Where does the light go when you turn the switch off?' A soul doesn't *go* anywhere; it just isn't there any more, because the things which made it possible have been taken away.

And yet, if a man was a good person and people loved him, even after his body has died and been buried, people will still remember him. They will talk about him and be slightly different people because of what he meant to them. And if they remember him and act differently because of it, maybe that is the answer to where his soul went.

When people we care about are alive, but physically distant from us, when a child's parents are at work or away on a trip, we can think of them and feel their presence and it is a little bit as if they were with us. This is what the power of love and memory can do. Let us be comforted by the thought that, even when people are dead, we can summon up memories of them and feel them close.

Harold S. Kushner

The Here and the Hereafter

Levi Yitzchak Horowitz, the first American-born Chasidic leader [...] was asked about his views on life after death. In characteristic fashion he began his response with a parable: Once upon a time there was a king who wanted to give a treat to the workers in his diamond mine. He told them that, for three hours only, they could keep for themselves all the diamonds they could pluck from the ground. Some got so excited that, as soon as they found a stone, they would polish it and fantasize what they would do with it once the three hours were over. Others just tried to collect as many diamonds as possible, leaving the polishing and the fantasising to later. Needless to say, these collected much more than the others. 'Why?' asks the rebbe, and answers: 'Because they used the time for what was meant to be.'

[...] We will not be helped if we spend all our time speculating about what we cannot know. It is not right for us to give assurances that no human being who has integrity and insight can dare to offer. It is far better for us to accept responsibility in life and to focus on what we can do here and now to make this world as rich and liveable as possible.

Not that there is nothing beyond this life, for our tradition is replete with references to *olam habah*, the world-to-come. But it insists that there is nothing you or I or any other human being can know about that world; all we can do is yearn and hope for it, not speculate about what it's like. To be responsible means to recognize our limitations as humans and accept our inability to see beyond the grave, and do the best we can now – in spite of the uncertainty [...]

And grieving will become virtually impossible. For the purpose of mourning is not to find answers about the afterlife, but to help mourners find their way back to this life. By affirming life as we experience it now, we can also build memorials for the dead. By carrying on where they left off, we can bestow meaning on their unfinished work and give purpose to ours – in the hope that those who follow us will, in turn, give meaning to our endeavour.

Dow Marmur

I Believe ...?

I have always believed that there is some spiritual life beyond the grave, that this earthly existence is not our only existence. Neither logic nor the details of the belief concern me. I will admit it is indeed a childish naiveté but I find it comforting. If I am proved right, I hope it will then turn out very well and that I am as content after life on earth as I have been during it.

If I am proved wrong and I should have listened all along to the voices of my lecturers at my first scientific degree course, who mocked my religious faith, then no matter. There will be nobody to laugh in my face at my naiveté. And the belief, briefly, will have comforted and sustained me as the days go by and I get nearer to death – long may such occurrence be delayed.

Andrew Goldstein

Kaddish *(for Marilyn)*

As long
as I speak
your name
you are
not dead

as long
as I think
your pain
I cannot
grieve

the granite marker
tells
your name
your age

the bleak horizon
scars
the barren hedge

as long
as I
you
are not dead

Hannah Kahn

Love Does Not Die

Everlasting God, help us to realize more and more that time
and space are not the measure of all things. Though our eyes
do not see, teach us to understand that the soul of our dear
ones is not cut off. Love does not die, and truth is stronger

than the grave. Just as our affection and the memory of the
good they did unite us with them at this time, so may our
trust in You lift us to the vision of the life that knows no
death.

Siddur Lev Chadash

They Alone are Left

They alone are left to me, they alone still faithful,
for now death can do no more to them.

At the bend of the road, at the close of day,
they gather around me silently, and walk by my side.

This is a bond nothing can ever loosen.
What I have lost: what I possess forever.

Rachel

Why Disquieted?

Why art thou cast down, my soul?
Why disquieted in me?
Feel'st thou not the Father nigh,
Him whose heart contains us all?
Lives no God for thee on high,
Loving while his judgements fall?
　　Look above!
　　God is love!
Why art thou cast down, my soul?
　　To the skies
　　Turn thine eyes;
Every tear on earth that flows,
God the world's great Ruler, knows.

Why art thou cast down my soul?
Why disquieted in me?
Was thy head in sorrow bending
'Neath the dreaded reaper's blight,
When thy loved ones were descending
In the darkness of death's night?
   Have no fear,
   God is near!
Be consoled, my soul, in God,
   Tears take flight,
   For in light
Walk thy dead on heaven's shore,
Blessed, blessed, evermore!

Why art thou cast down my soul?
Why disquieted in me?
Ever shall thy dead be living –
From the darkness of the tomb
God, thy Father, mercy-giving,
Take them to his heavenly home.
   Wilt thou trust
   God, the just?
Soul, my soul, be strong in God.
   God's with thee
   Eternally!
Then thy hopes shall be fulfilled
And thy heart's pain shall be stilled.

Liberal Jewish Prayer Book

Death Will Come

Death will come.
Its hand will not be stayed
even an instant; nor can we enter
into judgment with it.
Our question 'Why?'
will go unanswered.
But this does not mean
that we are helpless
in the face of death.

We can and we do rob
death of ultimate victory,
by living life
as long as it is ours to live.

To ask of death
that it never come
is futile, but it is not futility
to pray that when death comes for us,
it may take us from a world
one corner of which
is a little better
because we were there.

When we are dead,
and people weep for us and grieve,
let it be because
we touched their lives
with beauty and simplicity.
Let it not be said
that life was good to us,
but rather that we were good to life.

Jacob P. Rudin

16

Faith and the Power of Prayer

Psalm 27

The Eternal One is my light and my salvation
Whom should I fear?
The Eternal One is the strength of my life
Of whom shall I be afraid?
When those bent on evil draw near to slander me,
When foes threaten, they stumble and fall.
Though an army encamp against me my heart will not fear
Though war be waged against me my trust will still be firm.
One thing only do I ask of God
To dwell in the house of the Eternal One all the days of my
    life;
to behold the beauty of the Eternal God
to seek God in the sanctuary.
For God shelters me in the tabernacle in times of trouble
Hides me in the hidden places then sets me high upon a
    rock.

And now my head is held high above my enemies who
   surround me
Therefore in God's tent will I offer sacrifices of exultation
I will sing, I will play music with joy before God.
Eternal One, hear my voice when I call,
Take pity on me and answer me.
Come, my heart has said, seek God's presence.
I will seek Your presence, Eternal One.
Do not hide Your face from me, do not turn away Your
   servant in anger for You have been my help.
Do not cast me off or forsake me, O God my Saviour.
Even if my father and mother were to desert me
Eternal God, You will care for me still.
Eternal God, teach me Your ways, lead me in straight paths
Do not deliver me to those who hate me,
to those who bear false witness against me
and plan to do me harm.
You have caused me to believe: that I shall see the goodness
   of the Eternal One
in the land of the living.
Put your hope in the Eternal One,
be strong, let your heart take courage,
only wait for the Eternal God.

Machzor Ruach Chadashah

Hear Me O God – Kayla's Prayer

Listen to my voice,
O Lord our God
And God of my ancestors.

I lie here on the brink of life,
Seeking peace, seeking comfort, seeking You.
To You, O Lord, I call and to You, O Lord, I make my
   supplication.

Do not ignore my plea.
Let your mercy flow over me like the waters,
Let the record of my life be a bond between us,
Listen to my voice when I call,
Be gracious to me and answer me.

I have tried, O Lord, to help You complete creation,
I have carried Your yoke my whole life.
I have tried to do my best.
Count my effort for the good of my soul,
Forgive me for when I have stumbled on Your path.
I can do no more, let my family carry on after me,
Let others carry on after me.

Protector of the helpless, healer of the brokenhearted,
Protect my beloved family with whose soul my own is
    bound.
Their hearts depended upon mine,
Heal their hearts when they come to depend on You.

Let my soul rest forever under the wings of Your presences,
Grant me a share in the world-to-come.
I have tried to love You with all my heart and with all my
    soul,
And even though You come to take my soul,
Even though I don't know why You come,
Even though I'm angry at the way You take me,
For Your sake I will still proclaim:
Hear, O Israel, the Lord is our God, the Lord alone.
The Lord is with me, I shall not fear.

Lawrence Troster

Give Us Trust

O Lord our God, in our great need for light we look to You. The quick flight of our days impels us to look back with regret or ahead with misgiving. There are times when we are baffled by disorder, and times when we come to doubt life's value and meaning. When suffering and death strike at those we love, our pain and anger embitter us. Our faith fails us; we find it hard to trust in You.

Eternal Spirit, make Your presence felt among us. Help us to find the courage to affirm You and to do Your will, even when the shadows fall upon us. When our own weakness and the storms of life hide You from our sight, teach us that You are near to each one of us at all times, and especially when we strive to live truer, gentler, nobler lives. Give us trust, Lord; give us peace, and give us light. May our hearts find their rest in You.

Liberal Jewish Prayer Book

Give Us Hope

When evil darkens our world, give us light.
When despair numbs our souls, give us hope.

When we stumble and fall, lift us up.
When doubts assail us, give us faith.

When nothing seems sure, give us trust.
When ideals fade, give us vision.

When we lose our way, be our guide!
That we may find serenity in Your presence, and purpose
in doing Your will.

John D. Rayner

Eternal Love

We are loved by an unending love,
We are embraced by arms that find us
    even when we are hidden from ourselves.

We are touched by fingers that soothe us
    even when we are too proud for soothing.
We are counselled by voices that guide us
    even when we are too embittered to hear.
We are loved by an unending love.

We are supported by hands that uplift us
    even in the midst of a fall.
We are urged on by eyes that meet us
    even when we are too weak for meeting.
We are loved by an unending love.

Embraced, touched, soothed, and counselled ...
    ours are the arms, the fingers, the voices;
    ours are the hands, the eyes, the smiles.
We are loved by an unending love.

Blessed are you, Beloved One, who loves your people
    Israel.

Rami Shapiro

From Psalm 139

Whither can I go from Your spirit?
Whither can I flee from Your presence?
If I ascend to the heavens, You are there!
If I make my bed in the lower depths,
behold, You are there!
If I take up the wings of the morning,

and dwell on the ocean's farthest shore,
even there Your hand will lead me,
Your hand will hold me.
If I say: Surely darkness will conceal me,
night will hide me from view,
even the darkness is not too dark for You,
the night is clear as the day;
darkness is light to You.

Psalm 139.1–12

Do Not Be Afraid

As the Baal Shem Tov lay on his deathbed, his Chasidim stood about him and wept bitterly. He said: 'Let me see no tears on your faces; I am only going out of one door and in through another.' When the Baal Shem's son entered, and bent over his father, he received from the dying man the message which had become the watchword of his life: 'Remember this always: wherever you go, wherever you are, God is with you. Why, then, ever be afraid?'

Chasidic

From Psalm 71

As for me, I will hope always,
   and add to the many praises of You.
My mouth tells of your beneficence,
   of Your deliverance all day long,
   though I know not how to tell it.
I come with praise of Your mighty acts, Eternal;
   I celebrate your beneficence, Yours alone.
You have let me experience it, God,
   from my youth;

159

until now I have proclaimed Your wondrous
    deeds,
and even in ripe old age do not forsake me,
God,
until I proclaim Your strength to the next generation,
Your mighty acts, to all who are to come.

Psalm 71.14–18, 19a

To Say Kaddish

When death comes to the person you love,
you will go down to darkness and despair
and in the depths of loneliness will find
your naked soul, craven and cold.

You whose mind has considered and doubted,
whose heart has faltered and whose courage has failed,
will wring out the final personal word
from your stricken soul.

And death has no truth but this: I believe,
Death has no victory but this:
to rise from doubt and cold darkness
to magnify and hallow the name of God.

Ruth F. Brin

Kaddish

Yitgadal Ve-yitkadash Shemey Rabba ...
Magnified and sanctified be the great name of the One
    by whose will the world was created. May God's rule
    become effective in your lives, and in the life of
    the whole House of Israel. May it be so and let us say:
      Amen

May God's great name be praised to all eternity.

Blessed and praised; glorified, exalted and extolled;
    lauded, honoured and acclaimed be the name of the
    Holy One, who is ever to be praised, though far above
    the eulogies and songs of praise and consolation that
    human lips can utter; and let us say: Amen

May great peace descend from heaven, and abundant
    life be granted, to us and all Israel; and let us say: Amen

May the Most High, Source of perfect peace, grant
    peace to us, to all Israel, and to all humanity
      and let us say: Amen

Siddur Lev Chadash

Glossary

Aggadah	Hebrew, largely but not exclusively, rabbinic story-telling, mostly written by Palestinian Jews between the Second Temple and the end of the Talmudic era
Avot de Rabbi Natan	Hebrew, a work of aggadah written between 700 and 900 CE, often designated as a super-commentary/exposition of Pirkei Avot (see below)
The Ba-al Shem Tov	Hebrew, 'Master of the Good Name', the title given to Israel ben Eliezer, c.1698–1760 – the founder of Chasidism in the eighteenth century
Bris	Hebrew, 'circumcision'
Chasidim	Hebrew word meaning 'pious ones', the name given to very devout Jews, usually followers of a particular Tzaddik or Rebbe (see below)
Derekh eretz	Hebrew, 'the way of the land', but referring to common decency and respect for others
Elimelech of Lyzhensk	(1717–86) major Chasidic rabbi
Eshet Chayil	Hebrew, 'a woman of strength' (Proverbs 31.10–31)
Halachah	Hebrew, 'Jewish Law', including those laws found in the Torah and Rabbinic Literature
Havdalah	Hebrew, 'separation', the ceremony at the end of the Sabbath, marking a clear separation between the day of rest and the first day of the week

Hezekiah	King of Judah, reigned c.727–698 BCE
Kaddish	Aramaic, 'sanctification', the name of the prayer recited by Jews at funerals and Yahrzeits (see below)
Korach	the leader of a rebellious faction during the Israelites' wandering in the desert (Num. 16)
Mah Tov	Hebrew, 'how good', echoing the statement of the pagan seer Balaam in the book of Numbers, *Mah Tovu Ohalecha Ya-akov*, How goodly are your tents, O Jacob (Num. 24.5)
Mishnah	Hebrew, the primary legal text of the Jewish oral tradition, edited by Rabbi Judah the Prince, c.200 CE
Mitzvos	the Hebrew word for commandments, pronounced as *mitzvot* by Progressive Jews worldwide, Israelis, and Sephardi Jews
Nu	Yiddish, a word pronounced with a strong, interrogative inflection, meaning 'well???'
Pirkei Avot	Hebrew, 'Chapters of the Sages' or 'Ethics of the Fathers'; a collection of rabbinic aphorisms in the fourth tractate of the Mishnah, the first documentation of the Oral Law believed by traditional Jews to have been revealed to Moses on Mt Sinai at the same time as the Torah, the Written Law
Rabbi Meir	(c.139–63 CE) one of the foremost sages and legal traditionaries of the Mishnah
Rabbi Moshe ben Maimon	one of the greatest Jews who ever lived (1135–1204) otherwise known as Maimonides
Rabbi Simcha Bunim of Przysucha	(1765–1827) Chasidic Tzaddik (see below)
Rebbe	honorific title of a revered Chasidic rabbi

Seder	Hebrew 'order'; the name of the much loved ceremonial meal on the eve of the first day of Passover
Shamash	Hebrew, 'servant', applied to a synagogue beadle
The Shema	'Hear O Israel! The Eternal One is our God, the Eternal God is One' (Deuteronomy 6.4), the watchword of the Jewish faith proclaiming the unity of God, recited twice daily by the devout and if possible just before death
Shemini Atzeret	Hebrew, the eighth day of the festival of Sukkot (Tabernacles)
Shiv'ah	Hebrew, 'seven', but always used to connote the seven days of mourning immediately following a burial
Talmud	Hebrew, the great commentary on and exposition of the Mishnah (see above); there are two versions, the Jerusalem and the Babylonian, of which the latter is deemed authoritative
Tzaddik	Hebrew, 'Righteous One', the honorific title given to a great Chasidic Rabbi, often believed by his followers to influence God by his direct appeal
Yaakov Glatstein	(1896–1971) Polish-born Yiddish poet and literary critic
Yahrzeit	a German word universally used by Jews to denote the annual anniversary of the death of a loved one
Yekutiel	Yekutiel ben Isaac ibn Chasan, Jewish vizier of Muslim Saragossa, murdered in a palace coup in 1039 at the age of 100
Yitzhak Perlman	Israeli virtuoso violinist, afflicted with polio from the age of four
Yizkor	Hebrew, literally 'let him remember' but used as a title for a memorial prayer, and the memorial service on the Day of Atonement, Yom Kippur

Sources

Israel Abrahams	1858–1925. Leading British Jewish scholar, Reader in Talmud at Cambridge
Morris Adler	1906–66. American Conservative rabbi
Ronald Aigen	Canadian Conservative rabbi
Shifra Alon	Israeli poet
Yehuda Amichai	1924–2000. Israeli poet
Camille Shira Angel	American rabbi, spiritual leader to San Francisco's Congregation Sha'ar Zahav
Apocrypha	scriptural texts not included in the canon of the Hebrew Bible
Bradley Shavit Artson	American Conservative rabbi and writer
Elazar Azikri	1533–1600. Rabbi, kabbalist, poet and writer
Baal Shem Tov	1698–1760. Title meaning Master of the Good Name, awarded to Rabbi Israel ben Eliezer, the founder of Chasidism
Ellen Bass	American poet
Ben Sira	Apocryphal work, dating between 200–175 BCE
Chaim Nachman Bialik	1873–1934. Hebrew poet
Bible	The Hebrew Bible; texts usually based on the JPS or NRSV translations
Ruth F. Brin	1921–2009. American poet, liturgist and children's writer

Martin Buber	1878–1965. Austrian-born Israeli philosopher, educator and translator
Joseph Caro	1488–1575, author of the *Shulchan Arukh*, the last great code of Jewish Law
Eric J. Cassell	American doctor and Emeritus Professor of Public Health, Cornell University
Samuel Chiel	1927–2013, American Conservative rabbi
Henry Dreher	American writer on health issues
Zevi Hirsch Edelman	1805–58. Russian Hebraist and scholar
Abraham ibn Ezra	c.1089–1164. Philosopher, bible commentator, poet and linguist
Elaine Feinstein	British writer, poet and playwright
Edward Field	American poet and writer
Alvin I. Fine	1916–99. American Reform rabbi
Nancy Flam	American Reform rabbi
Forms of Prayer	Liturgy of the Reform Movement in Great Britain
Viktor E. Frankl	1905–97. Austrian-born neurologist, psychiatrist and Holocaust survivor
Seymour Freedman	American-Israeli writer and poet
Solomon B. Freehof	1892–1990. American Reform rabbi, scholar and pre-eminent author of Reform Responsa
Solomon ibn Gabirol	c.1021–58. Pre-eminent Hebrew poet, and philosopher of the Golden Age of Spain
Laura Crafton Gilpin	1950–2007. American poet, nurse and advocate for patients' rights
Leah Goldberg	1911–70. Poet and translator
Kalie Golden	American poet
David Goldstein	1933–87. British Liberal rabbi, translator and oriental scholar
Earl A. Grollman	American rabbi and pioneer in crisis intervention

Jacob L. Halevi	1900–88. American Reform rabbi and philosopher
Judah Halevi	1075–1141. Spanish poet and philosopher
Harry Halpern	1899–1981. American Conservative rabbi and educator
M. Leivick Halpin	1888–1962. Russian-born American Yiddish poet
Shmuel Ha-Nagid	993–1056. Spanish poet, rabbinic scholar, politician and general in Muslim Granada
Abraham Joshua Heschel	1907–72. Rabbi, teacher and civil rights activist, and pre-eminent Jewish philosopher of the twentieth century
Barry W. Holtz	Theodore and Florence Baumritter Professor of Jewish Education at the Jewish Theological Seminary in New York
David Ignatow	1914–97. American poet
Morris Joseph	1848–1930. British Reform rabbi and theologian
Hannah Kahn	1911–88. American poet
Elana Kanter	American Reform rabbi
Judy Katz	American writer
Karyn Kedar	American Reform rabbi
A. M. Klein	1909–72. Canadian poet, novelist and journalist
Moyshe Kulbak	1896–1937. Belarus-born poet and writer
Harold S. Kushner	American Conservative rabbi and best-selling author
Lawrence Kushner	American Reform rabbi and mystic
Steven Z. Leder	American rabbi and author
Joseph Leftwich	1892–1984. British poet, biographer and literary critic
Mani Leib	1883–1953. Ukrainian-born American Yiddish poet
Richard N. Levy	American rabbi and educator

Liberal Jewish Prayer Book	the first prayer book of English Liberal Judaism, edited by Rabbi Dr Israel I. Mattuck
Anna Lichtenberg	Member of San Francisco's Congregation Sha'ar Zahav
Joshua Loth Liebman	1907–48. American rabbi and prolific author
Jeffrey Lilly	American poet
Machzor	prayer book for the High Holy Days and the Pilgrimage Festivals
Machzor Ruach Chadashah	the current High Holy Day prayer book of English Liberal Judaism
Moses Maimonides	1135–1204. Rabbi, physician and philosopher
Dow Marmur	Polish-born Reform rabbi
Israel I. Mattuck	1883–1954. First rabbi of English Liberal Judaism
Robert Mezey	American poet and translator
Midrash	the corpus of rabbinic homiletical Bible interpretation
Robert Mills	American Jewish community worker and poet
Mishnah	the primary text of Jewish Oral Law
Agi Mishol	Hungarian-born Israeli poet
Nachman of Bratslav	1772–1810. Hasidic rabbi and grandson of the Baal Shem Tov
Linda Pastan	American poet
Esther Raab	1894–1981. Israeli poet
Rachel	1890–1931. Pen name of Rachel Bluwstein Sela, Hebrew poet
Andrew Ramer	American writer
John D. Rayner	1924–2005. Pre-eminent Liberal rabbi, scholar, theologian and liturgist
Abraham Reisen	Yiddish poet

Charles Reznikoff	1894–1976. American poet
Adrienne Rich	1929–2012. American poet, essayist and feminist
Jack Riemer	American rabbi, liturgist and anthologist
Joseph Rolnick	1879–1955. Russian-born American poet
Menachem Rosensaft	American attorney, leader of the Second Generation movement
Efraim M. Rosenzweig	American Conservative rabbi
Walter Rothschild	British Reform rabbi
Jacob P. Rudin	1902–82. American Reform rabbi
Tuviah Ruebner	Israeli poet, editor and writer
Robert Saks	American Reform rabbi
Israel Salanter	1810–83. Rabbi, founder of the Musar movement in orthodox Judaism
Harold M. Schulweis	American Conservative rabbi, writer and poet
Hannah Senesh	1921–44. Hungarian-born Israeli agent parachuted back into Nazi-occupied Hungary, captured, tortured and murdered by the Nazis
Rami Shapiro	American Reform rabbi and author
Joshua ibn Shuaib	early fourteenth-century Spanish preacher and scholar
Siddur Lev Chadash	the current daily, Sabbath and Festival prayer book of English Liberal Judaism
Danny Siegel	American Conservative rabbi and poet
Arlene Stein	American sociologist and activist
Milton Steinberg	American Conservative rabbi, philosopher, theologian and novelist
Chaim Stern	1930–2001. American Reform rabbi and liturgist
Ilse Sternberger	1914–2002. German-born poet, author and teacher

Michael Strassfeld	1903–50. American Reconstructionist rabbi and author
Talmud	the commentary to the Mishnah, found in two versions, the Jerusalem and the Babylonian, redacted between the third and sixth centuries CE
Joseph Telushkin	American Orthodox rabbi and author
Lawrence Troster	American Conservative rabbi
Michael Tyler	editor, *Siddur Sha'ar Zahav*, San Francisco
David Vogel	1891–1944. Russian-born Hebrew poet, murdered in Auschwitz
Albert Vorspan	leading American Reform lay leader and social activist
Jonathan Wittenberg	British Conservative rabbi
Ron Wolfson	American academic
David Wolpe	American Conservative rabbi
Levi Yitzchak of Berditchev	1740–1810. Chasidic rabbi and leader
Israel Zangwill	1864–1926. British writer and humourist

Copyright Acknowledgements

Every effort has been made to secure copyright permissions from the authors cited or their publisher. We acknowledge with gratitude the permissions we have received and will be happy to rectify any errors of omission in subsequent printings.

The Editors

1 The Pain of Life

'The Meaning of Life' by Viktor E. Frankl. From *Man's Search for Meaning* © 1959, 1962, 1984, 1992 by Viktor E. Frankl. Reprinted by permission of Beacon Press, Boston

'No Easy Answer' by Joseph Telushkin. Copyright © 1997 by Joseph Telushkin. From *Biblical Literacy: Most Important People, Events of the Hebrew Bible* by Joseph Telushkin, William Morrow and Company Inc., a division of HarperCollins US

'Spare Those I Love' by Tuviah Ruebner; from *Were Our Mouths Filled with Song* by Eric L. Friedland, © 1997. Reprinted by permission of the University of Pittsburg Press/Hebrew Union College Press

'The Great Sad One' by Robert Mezey from *Collected Poems 1952–1999*. Copyright © 1965, 2000 Robert Mezey. Reprinted with the permission of The Permissions Company, Inc., on behalf of the University of Arkansas Press, www.uapress.com

'Gray Good-Bye' by Danny Siegel ©, reprinted by permission of the author; from *Unlocked Doors*, Townhouse Press, 1983

'The Storms of Life' by Israel I. Mattuck. Reprinted by permission of Liberal Judaism, The Montagu Centre, 21 Maple Street, London W1T 4BE, www.liberaljudaism.org

'Fear and Loneliness' from *Siddur Lev Chadash*. Reprinted by permission of Liberal Judaism, as above

2 Patience and Fortitude

'Give Me Courage' from *The Liberal Jewish Prayer Book*. Reprinted by permission of Liberal Judaism, as previously

'I Shall Live' by Elana Kanter. Copyright © Elana Kanter. First published in *Sh'ma: A Journal of Jewish Ideas*, volume 28, no. 554

'A Prayer' by Abraham Reisen, translation copyright © Leonard Woolf. Reprinted by kind permission of the translator

'In Times of Darkness' by Jacob L. Halevi. © Jacob L. Halevi, from *The Journal of Reform Judaism*, Central Conference of American Rabbis, volume 23, Summer, 1976

'When Bad Things Happen' by Harold S. Kushner. Excerpt from *When Bad Things Happen to Good People* by Harold S. Kushner, copyright © 1981 by Harold S. Kushner. Used by permission of Schocken Books, an imprint of the Knopf Doubleday Publishing Group, a division of Random House LLC. All rights reserved

3 Illness

'Loss of Health' by Earl A. Grollman. *Caring and Coping when Your Loved One is Ill*. Copyright © 1995 Earl A Grollman. Reprinted by permission of Beacon Press, Boston.

'My Last Cancer Treatment' by David Wolpe. Reprinted by permission of the author

'Prayer for Healing' from *Siddur Lev Chadash*. Reprinted by permission of Liberal Judaism, as previously

'As One Approaches Surgery (or Crisis)' by Chaim Stern (from unpublished papers)

'Keeping Perspective' by Chaim Stern, as above

ACKNOWLEDGEMENTS

'The Long Days', excerpt from *Gates of Healing: A Message of Comfort and Hope* © 1988, Central Conference of American Rabbis. Used by permission. All rights reserved

'For Those Living with a Chronic Illness' by Jeffrey Lilly. © 2008 by Jeffrey Lilly. Excerpted from *Siddur Sha'ar Zahav*. Copyright © Congregation Sha'ar Zahav, San Francisco, CA, reprinted with permission. All rights reserved. http://shaarzahav.org

'To Wake Up in the Hospital Early in the Morning' by Rachel. Translation © Benjamin Harshav, cited in *Jewish Insights into Death and Mourning*, edited by Jack Riemer and Sherwin B. Nuland, Syracuse University Press, 2002

'Whatever Will Come' by Samuel Chiel and Henry Dreher. Copyright © 2007 Samuel Chiel and Henry Dreher, from *The Healing Power of Psalms: Renewal, Hope and Acceptance from the World's Most Beloved Ancient Verses*. Reprinted by permission of Da Capo Press, a member of the Perseus Book Group

'Books or People' by Harold M. Schulweis. From Harold M. Schulweis, *Finding Each Other in Judaism* (New York: UAHC Press, 2001). Reprinted with permission of URJ Press. All rights reserved

'May I Not Soon Forget: Postoperative Prayer' by Harold M. Schulweis, as above

4 Healing

'The Baal Shem Tov was Passing' © Rami Shapiro. Reprinted by permission of the author

'When I suffer' by Anna Lichtenberg and Michael Tyler. *Meditative Weekday Amidah*, copyright © 2008 by Anna Lichtenberg and Michael Tyler. Excerpted from *Siddur Sha'ar Zahav*. Copyright © Congregation Sha'ar Zahav, San Francisco, CA, reprinted with permission. All rights reserved. http://shaarzahav.org

'Heal Me' by Judah Halevi, translated by David Goldstein. Reprinted by permission of Berry Goldstein

'For Caregivers' by Andrew Ramer. Copyright © 2008 by Andrew Ramer. Excerpted from *Siddur Sha'ar Zahav*. Copyright © Congregation Sha'ar Zahav, San Francisco, CA, reprinted with permission. All rights reserved. http://shaarzahav.org

'For Life' by Harold M. Schulweis, as previously

'Playing with Three Strings' by Harold M. Schulweis, as previously

'The Power of Music' by Camille Shira Angel. *Songs, Stories, Humor*, copyright © 2008 by Camille Shira Angel. Excerpted from *Siddur Sha'ar Zahav*. Copyright © Congregation Sha'ar Zahav, San Francisco, CA, reprinted with permission. All rights reserved. http://shaarzahav.org

'Blessing for Our Bodies', excerpted from *Siddur Sha'ar Zahav*. Copyright © Congregation Sha'ar Zahav, San Francisco, CA, reprinted with permission. All rights reserved. http://shaarzahav.org

'God waits' by Shifra Alon. Translated by Chaim Stern. Reprinted by permission of Liberal Judaism, as previously

5 Growing Older

'Paradoxes' by Ilse Naumann Sternberger, published in *The Journal of Reform Judaism*, Central Conference of American Rabbis, volume 31, 1984

'Looking Back' by Leah Goldberg. Translated by Chaim Stern, reprinted by permission of Liberal Judaism, as previously

'A Victory' by John D. Rayner. Reprinted by permission of Liberal Judaism, as above

'Children of a Book' by Robert Mills, published in *The Journal of Reform Judaism*, Central Conference of American Rabbis, Winter, 1980

'The Army of Old Age' by Shmuel Hanagid, translated by David Goldstein, reprinted by permission of Berry Goldstein

'Senility' by Danny Siegel. © As previously, from *Between Dust and Dance*, Townhouse Press, 1978

'Love Sometimes Dies' by Danny Siegel. © As previously, from *Nine Entered Paradise Alive*, Townhouse Press, 1980

'Place Me Under Your Wing' by Chaim N. Bialik, English translation copyright © 1979 Gabriel Levin, from *Voices within the Ark: The Modern Jewish Poets. An International Anthology* edited by Howard

ACKNOWLEDGEMENTS

Schwartz and Anthony Rudolf. Copyright © 1980 by Howard Schwartz and Anthony Rudolf.

'Yahrzeit Poem' by Barry W. Holtz. It appeared originally in *Response* Magazine #22, Summer 1974

'For Caregivers of Ailing or Aged Parents' by Andrew Ramer. Copyright © 2008 by Andrew Ramer. Excerpted from *Siddur Sha'ar Zahav*. Copyright © Congregation Sha'ar Zahav, San Francisco, CA, reprinted with permission. All rights reserved. http://shaarzahav.org

'Valentine for a Middle-Aged Spouse' by Elaine Feinstein. © Elaine Feinstein and Carcanet Press Ltd; from *Collected Poems and Translations*, 2002

'When I was Growing Up' by David Vogel. A. C. Jacobs, *Collected Poems and Selected Translations*, edited by Anthony Rudolf and John Rety, published by Menard Press/Hearing Eye, London 1996. © Sheila V. Gilbert, reprinted with permission of the copyright holder

6 Contemplating Mortality

'Birth is a Beginning' by Alvin I. Fine. Excerpt from *Gates of Repentance*, edited by Chaim Stern © 1978 by Central Conference of American Rabbis. Used by permission. All rights reserved

'A Life of Poetry' by Yehuda Amichai, translated by Benjamin Harshav. © Benjamin Harshav, from *Yehuda Amichai: A Life of Poetry, 1948–1994*, HarperCollins (USA), 1998

'Man Runs Towards the Grave' by Shmuel Hanagid, translated by David Goldstein. Reprinted with the permission of Berry Goldstein

'The Pull of Gravity' by Agi Mishol. Translated by Lisa Katz, © Agi Mishol, from *Look There: New and Selected Poems*, Gray Wolf Press, St. Paul, Minnesota, 2002

'Fear of Death' by Harold M. Schulweis, as previously

'If Not Now, When?' by Bradley Shavit Artson. Reprinted by permission of the author.

'Autumn is Near and Memory of My Parents' by Yehuda Amichai, translated by Benjamin Harshav. © Benjamin Harshav, from *Yehuda Amichai: A Life of Poetry, 1948–1994*, HarperCollins (USA), 1998

'Wounded Lions' by Shmuel Hanagid, translated by Charles H. Middleburgh © Rabbi Dr Charles H. Middleburgh 2010

'Is It Really the End?' by Rachel. Translated by Chaim Stern. Reprinted by permission of Liberal Judaism, as previously

7 Death and Dying

'Use Life Well' by Lawrence Kushner. From *I'm God, You're Not: Observations on Organized Religion and Other Disguises of the Ego*. Jewish Lights Publishing, www.jewishlights.com

'To Part Humbly' by Jonathan Wittenberg. Copyright © Jonathan Wittenberg, 2001. From *The Eternal Journey*, published by Joseph's Bookstore, London. Reprinted with the permission of the author and publisher

'Above Everything' by David Ignatow; from *Against the Evidence: Selected Poems 1934–1994*, © 1993 by David Ignatow. Reprinted by permission of Wesleyan University Press

'This Last Today' by Efraim M. Rosenzweig. From *Genizah Fragments*, Etzem Press, 1983

'Your Hand in Mine' by Efraim M. Rosenzweig, as above

'Our Hold on Life' by Solomon B. Freehof. © 1940, The Central Conference of American Rabbis, *Union Prayer Book*, volume 1, 1961

'It is Never Too Late' by Harold M. Schulweis, as previously

'Sacks of Almonds' by Esther Raab. © all rights reserved to Author and ACUM

'Letting Go' by Nancy Flam. © Nancy Flam, Institute for Jewish Spirituality, cited in *Jewish Insights into Death and Mourning*, eds. Jack Riemer and Sherwin B. Nuland, Random House Inc., 1995

'Life and Death' by Alvin I. Fine. From *'Speak to the Heart': Anthology of Readings and Statements for Funeral and Memorial Services*, Ad Art Publishing Company, 1956

'My Grandmother' by Moyshe Kulbak from *An Anthology of Modern Yiddish Literature*, ed. Joseph Leftwich. Copyright © 1974 in the Netherlands, Mouton and Co, N.V. Publishers, The Hague

'How We Bury' by Ron Wolfson. From *A Time to Mourn: A Time to Comfort*. Copyright © 1993 The Federation of Jewish Men's Clubs, 475 Riverside Drive, Suite 244, New York, NY 10115

'From a Mother to Her Girls' by Karyn Kedar. *The Bridge to Forgiveness: Stories and Prayers for Finding God and Restoring Wholeness*. Jewish Lights Publishing, www.jewishlights.com

8 A Coda: Death Before Their Time

'After a Stillbirth' by Walter Rothschild. Reprinted by permission of the author

'On the Death of His Son Isaac' by Abraham ibn Ezra, translated by David Goldstein. Reprinted by permission of Berry Goldstein.

'Bittersweet: In Memory of a Child' by Harold M. Schulweis, as previously

'For Parents Who Mourn a Child' by Chaim Stern. Excerpt from *On the Doorposts of Your House* by Chaim Stern © 1994, 2010 by Central Conference of American Rabbis. Used by permission. All rights reserved

'I cannot see you' by Charles Middleburgh, copyright © 2014 Rabbi Dr Charles H. Middleburgh

9 Grieving

'Peace of Mind: Grief's Slow Wisdom' by Joshua Loth Liebman. Copyright © 1946 by Joshua Loth Liebman, from *Peace of Mind*, Kensington Publishing Corp., 1998

'Three Laws for Governing Grief' by Joshua Loth Liebman, as above

'For My Mother' by Ruth F. Brin, from *A Time to Search: Poems and Prayers for Our Day*, Jonathan David Company, 1959

'The Five Stages of Grief' by Linda Pastan. Copyright © Linda Pastan 1978, from *The Five Stages of Grief*, W.W. Norton, 1978

'After My Death' by Chaim Nachman Bialik. From *Voices Within the Ark: The Modern Jewish Poets. An International Anthology* edited by Howard Schwartz and Anthony Rudolf. Copyright © 1980 by Howard Schwartz and Anthony Rudolf. © Sheila V. Gilbert, reprinted with permission of the copyright holder

'For My Daughter on Her Twenty-First Birthday' by Ellen Bass, from *Mules of Love*. Copyright © 2002 by Ellen Bass. Reprinted with the permission of The Permissions Company, Inc., on behalf of BOA Editions Ltd., www.boaeditions.org

From 'Look There' by Agi Mishol, as previously

'In Mourning for Yekutiel' by Solomon ibn Gabirol. Translated by David Goldstein, reprinted by permission of Berry Goldstein

'They say "Time Heals"' by Seymour Freedman. From *Mourning for My Father*, Field Publishing House 1989. © Seymour Freedman

'What We Really Lose' by Jonathan Wittenberg, as previously

10 Words of Comfort

'If We Choose Rightly' by Chaim Stern. From *Gates of Prayer*, as previously

'Coronary Connections' by Harold M. Schulweis, as previously

'God Gives Us Strength' by Harold S. Kushner, as previously

'I am Older Now' by Harold M. Schulweis, as previously

'Consolation' by Israel I. Mattuck. Reprinted by permission of Liberal Judaism, as previously

'Life on Earth' by the Editors, based on an original piece by Solomon B. Freehof

'A Child's Comfort' by Lawrence Kushner. From *I'm God, You're Not: Observations on Organized Religion and Other Disguises of the Ego*. Jewish Lights Publishing, www.jewishlights.com

'Conclusion of Shiv'ah' from *The Bond of Life: A Book for Mourners*, edited by Jules Harlow, 1983, reprinted with the permission of the Rabbinical Assembly

11 Legacy

'When Bad Things Happen to Good People' by Harold S. Kushner. Excerpt from *When Bad Things Happen to Good People* by Harold S. Kushner, copyright © 1981 by Harold S. Kushner. Used by permission of Schocken Books, an imprint of the Knopf Doubleday Publishing Group, a division of Random House LLC. All rights reserved

'The Dead Go On Living' by Laura Gilpin. From *The Hocus Pocus of the Universe*, copyright © 1977 by Laura Gilpin. Used by permission of Doubleday, an imprint of the Knopf Doubleday Publishing Group, a division of Random House LLC. All rights reserved

'When Our World is not Complete' by Richard N. Levy. From *Gates of Prayer*, edited by Chaim Stern. Copyright © 1975 Central Conference of American Rabbis. All rights reserved

'To Love and Lose' by Chaim Stern. From *Mishkan Tefillah*, Copyright © 2007, Central Conference of American Rabbis. All rights reserved

'Life is a Candle' by Chaim Stern. From *Mishkan Tefillah*, as above

'The Ethical Will' by Albert Vorspan. From *Jewish Values and Social Crisis: A Casebook for Social Action*. Copyright © Albert Vorspan 1968, UAHC/URJ Press, reprinted by permission of URJ Press

'The Essential Me' by Harold S. Kushner from *When Children Ask About God: A Guide for Parents Who Don't Always Know All The Answers* by Harold Kushner. Copyright © 1971, 1989 by Harold S. Kushner, used by permission of Schocken Books, an imprint of the Knopf Doubleday Publishing Group, a division of Random House LLC. All rights reserved

'Long Gone' by Edward Field. © Copyright Edward Field, reprinted by permission of the author

12 Gratitude

'An Alternative Psalm IV' by Danny Siegel, as above

'What is Good Cannot Perish' by Chaim Stern. Reprinted by permission of Liberal Judaism, as previously

13 Memory

ACKNOWLEDGEMENTS

Reprinted by permission of Houghton Mifflin Harcourt Publishing Company. All rights reserved

'Yahrzeit Candle' by Efraim M. Rosenzweig, as previously

14 Coda 2: Painful Memories

'A Yizkor Meditation' by Robert Saks, from *Yizkor for Festivals*, ed. Edward Feld, © 2011 The Rabbinical Assembly Inc. Reprinted with the permission of the Rabbinical Assembly

'My Mother' by Kalie Golden. © Kalie Golden, taken from *The Journal of Reform Judaism*, Central Conference of American Rabbis, Winter 1985

'Tattered Kaddish' by Adrienne Rich. Copyright © 2013 by The Adrienne Rich Literary Trust. Copyright © 1991 Adrienne Rich, from *Later Poems: Selected and New, 1971–2012* by Adrienne Rich. Used by permission of W.W. Norton & Company, Inc.

15 Immortality and Life After Death

'Where Do People Go When They Die?' by Harold S. Kushner. Excerpt from *When Children Ask About God* by Harold S. Kushner, copyright © 1989 by Harold S Kushner. Used by permission of Schocken Books, an imprint of the Knopf Doubleday Publishing Group, a division of Random House LLC. All rights reserved

'The Here and the Hereafter' by Dow Marmur. Reprinted by permission of the author

'I believe' by Andrew Goldstein. Copyright © Rabbi Dr Andrew Goldstein, 2014

'Kaddish (for Marilyn)' by Hannah Kahn. From *The Journal of Reform Judaism*, Central Conference of American Rabbis, Spring 2004

'They Alone are Left' by Rachel. Translated by Robert Mezey, © 1976 Robert Mezey; from *Voices Within The Ark: The Modern Jewish Poets. An International Anthology* edited by Howard Schwartz and Anthony Rudolf. Copyright © 1980 by Howard Schwartz and Anthony Rudolf, Avon Books

16 Faith and the Power of Prayer